# THE SILENT THOUGHT

# THE SILENT THOUGHT

*America in Crisis*

## CHARLIE WURZ

ARCHWAY
PUBLISHING

Archway Publishing books may be ordered through booksellers or by contacting:

Archway Publishing
1663 Liberty Drive
Bloomington, IN 47403
www.archwaypublishing.com
1 (888) 242-5904

Because of the dynamic nature of the Internet, any web addresses or
links contained in this book may have changed since publication and may
no longer be valid. The views expressed in this work are solely those
of the author and do not necessarily reflect the views of the publisher,
and the publisher hereby disclaims any responsibility for them.

Any people depicted in stock imagery provided by Thinkstock are models,
and such images are being used for illustrative purposes only.
Certain stock imagery © Thinkstock.

ISBN: 978-1-4808-2753-0 (sc)
ISBN: 978-1-4808-2754-7 (hc)
ISBN: 978-1-4808-2755-4 (e)

Library of Congress Control Number: 2016901787

Print information available on the last page.

Archway Publishing rev. date: 02/15/2016

# CONTENTS

# PREFACE

Silent thought!

What is it? And what do we do about it?

My reason for writing this book is rooted in my determination to understand what promotes thought, or the lack of thought altogether, and why thought does not progress to expression in either word or action.

Then my goal is to examine how this affects a variety of challenges facing our nation, challenges, which I believe are in a state of crisis.

When we consider what the silent thought is, it is important to see the implications of taking or not taking a thought to verbal expression and/or action.

Think of all the great improvements to our quality of life and whether these would be possible if our thoughts were not articulated or acted on, resulting in a wide variety of positive changes in our daily lives. Conversely, examine how incorrect thought has had adverse effects on human lives.

While silent thoughts can affect many aspects of our lives, including family, work, social relationships, and so forth, I prefer to examine how the silent thought affects politics in American life.

Here are some of the concepts I explore:

- Why do many people ignore thoughts regarding politics and instead accept sound bites from others to form their opinions?

- Does the American political system exploit silent thought?

- Is silent thought found in all segments of American society?

- What can be done to promote thought and expression?

- Who benefits the most or the least from silent thought?

We are approaching a critical crossroads in the American way of life, and the 2016 presidential election will have profound consequences. That encouraged me to write this book and hopefully inspire people to reexamine their thought processes and their resulting expressions and actions.

I have tried to write this book as a discussion with the reader in an attempt to provoke thought and promote a better understanding and perspective on how interconnected our daily lives are with American politics.

I will not cite countless statistics or the comments of others. My hope is that this book will prompt readers to search out relevant data to either support or refute my assertions and then form their own thoughtful and analytical opinions, no longer casually accepting the opinions of others, and also resisting the tendency of silent thought.

I am very concerned that many younger Americans, perhaps the so-called millennials, let's say those between eighteen and thirty-five years old, might take the greatness of this nation for granted, meaning they might think our way life is so rooted that it is there forever.

This could also be true for some in generation X, those thirty-five to fifty years old. This segment might be working toward their goals, building families, identifying with a particular political ideology, and accepting the status quo.

Some in my generation, baby boomers, let's say fifty-one to seventy and older, accept the status quo as well and might also believe there is insufficient time left for them to effect any change.

They might also believe that they have accomplished their goals, accepting the status quo and looking toward retirement. They might be choosing to let younger generations deal with it.

I make these assertions with concern, not criticism.

I encourage all of us to stay involved in the political process. The single greatest action every American can take is to vote—and vote as a well-informed citizen.

I believe our younger generations are in the best position to propel the changes we need now in America. Not to mention, they have the most at stake as they start or are in the early and middle stages of their journeys through life. However, they can be the most distracted.

At times, we all fail to identify the warning signs, which are more disguised now than ever before in our country. All of us should realize that America's greatness has never been at greater risk, for many reasons that we will discuss in detail throughout this book.

My greatest hope is that this book will reach the many Americans who have never considered thought in the way I will explain it and all too often just accept everything as it is.

The first two chapters deal with spontaneous and targeted thought, providing examples of each and how the concept of silent thought interconnects with both.

In chapters 3 through 8, I talk about several crises currently facing America and discuss how silent thought can have a negative influence on these major challenges facing every American.

Those crises are the following:

- leadership in America

- political correctness

- race relations in America

- politics in America

- open borders and immigration

Throughout this book, I also provide alternatives and solutions to combat the negative consequences of silent thought.

I have not written this book from any specific political perspective, such as any political party—democrat, republican, liberal, libertarian, conservative, or any other affiliation. Rather, I have written this book from an American perspective, in a very simple and straightforward approach.

Silent thought can be either a choice to not think about a topic at all or a choice to accept a narrow opinion and not apply any critical thought to the topic, such as politics.

This occurs when adopting a sound bite that may sound very convincing, depending on your perspective, but lacks any critical analysis.

Let's face it—the average citizen finds politics to be boring, not worth the time to worry about, and many feel it will never change, so why spend their valuable time on it when they can engage in so many other enjoyable topics and activities?

Politicians know this and certainly exploit this apathy by taking advantage of silent thought and then by targeting our thought with their agendas, which may or may not be in our best interest.

If we simply accept their points of view without any critical thought and analysis, we are choosing to sit on the sidelines. This will only continue and worsen until we decide as a unified country to change our political system.

So who benefits the most and least without a change of course is pretty obvious, isn't it!

Our American political system exploits silent thought and the lack of desire by a majority in this country who just don't feel the need to participate in our political system other than voting, sometimes not voting at all, other times only voting in a national presidential election, or vice versa, in a local contest or referendum and never really noticing a national political contest.

Sure, many of us complain about politics and politicians all the time, but what are we doing other than just that? The solutions are not easy, and it is simpler to just send these concerns to the brain's silent thought chamber and move on.

Silent thought is found in all walks of life, irrespective of your education level, financial situation, political party affiliation, or age. However, it appears in varying degrees within these segments.

Please remember that just because someone is a politician at the highest level of government does not mean he or she is someone of great intelligence. In many cases, it is just the opposite. Never assume that a politician is smarter than you, the American public.

In fact, politicians' incompetence and arrogance have not only caused these crises but also pushed the solutions further from reach!

These so-called political leaders in Washington, DC, are failing America and have placed the future of this great nation in jeopardy.

The solutions to solving these crises reside in the strength of every American, not in our local and national politicians who, as you will see, have no interest in facing these challenges.

My strongest desire is that America become a nation of leaders and then, as leaders, reestablish the greatness of America and all of its citizens.

I hope my readers find this book to be a quick read and one that stimulates their thought processes in ways that they may have not considered before.

So let's begin—and please keep an open mind, as the country we all love is at great risk.

# Chapter 1

# SPONTANEOUS THOUGHT

How many different ways can silent thought be described? Many! Let's start with the spontaneous thoughts that enter our brain. We briefly think about them, and they often exit our brain very quickly. This could be considered daydreaming or could be some of the most important thoughts of our lives and potentially influence the people closely tied to our individual lives.

Oftentimes we ask ourselves what that last thought was. *I know it had something to do with X, but I cannot remember it fully.* These occasions can be very frustrating, because we think, *Wow! That was really enlightening,* but we just can't remember its entire value.

What I will not do in this book is attempt to be technical about our brain's complicated design and how it processes thought. I will try to talk about everyday experiences and how valuable our thought process is to our daily journey from the time we wake until we fall asleep. Thought during sleep is a totally different process.

How many times have you noticed how fleeting thought can be? It can be very frustrating, with distraction after distraction taking from us from one thought to another, and we are sometimes not able to remember what might have been a very valuable thought.

Writing this book is very challenging because as I write each word, sentence, and paragraph, I am constantly thinking about what I am writing as well as all the other daily facets of my life, including family, work, goals, and on and on. I cannot even imagine how many spontaneous thoughts one has in the course of a day. I am sure the professionals in this field may have an idea, and it must be substantial. We have to ask ourselves how one makes it through the workday, irrespective of what we do in the workplace, with all of these distractions.

Spontaneous thought can be problematic if it is allowed to consume our day and not allow us to focus on the critical thought needed in order to perform at all levels in the workplace, home, family, and social settings.

Have you ever sat in a coffee shop for any period of time and realized how many different thoughts you experience as you interact silently with other people and their actions or appearances? If you are sitting or standing close enough to hear others speaking—not eavesdropping, just casual instances of overhearing others—you receive even more thought triggers, continuously causing you to have spontaneous thoughts, either very quickly leaving your consciousness or taking more of your thinking and consideration.

This same experience can happen during a business meeting, riding the subway or bus, driving, sitting or walking in a park, during a round of golf, just about everywhere.

So what do we do about this as we navigate through our day? Do we consider these thought triggers as a nuisance and a distraction, or we do we enjoy the stimulus it produces inside of our brains, resulting in all sorts of analysis, certainly not scientific in most cases?

I guess this is the idea behind people watching and the reason we do it, some more than others.

How many different thoughts have you just had while reading the last several paragraphs in this book? I hope they were positive and encouraged you to keep reading.

Ask yourself:

- What benefit can be derived from spontaneous thought?

- Is this innocent curiosity, or are we nosy?

- Do we form opinions from any of these spontaneous thoughts?

I will give you my answers to these questions.

In order to fully understand what causes silent thought, we certainly need to experience spontaneous thought, so we can experience the benefits derived from spontaneous interactions of thought and analysis.

I believe this is just innocent curiosity, and with just a little inquisitiveness (possibly being nosy), it can expose us to the many great facets of our human existence.

Most definitely we form opinions from these spontaneous thoughts. These opinions can have a wide range of importance, from insignificant to opinions that have a significant impact on our lives and that of every other person we encounter.

One trigger I have not mentioned—but probably most influences spontaneous thought—is the media impact to our thought process. This comes at us in many forms, such as print, television (both cable and broadcast), Internet via news and blog sites, social sites, radio, and advertising of all types.

Let's first think about the media in terms of the so-called mainstream media outlets, such as the major network news channels.

Ask yourself:

- Do we get unbiased news of the day or opinions?

- Should we rely solely on these?

- Are the news anchors presenting unfiltered news, or are they following an agenda, whether that agenda be personal or driven by network executives?

- More specifically, are these news presenters more concerned with their own personal ambitions, including political and/or social agendas, or are they simply there to inform the public with factual news accounts?

If you are old enough, you can recall when the major networks—NBC, CBS, and ABC—and their local affiliate stations were the primary news sources for the American public. We now have an abundance of cable broadcasts and Internet sites that provide many choices for our news consumption.

These sources can be found in many forms, including factual news, opinion talk shows, and Internet forums. Unfortunately, many so-called news sources provide only short sound bites that they believe will find their way into our consciousness.

To rely only on quick sound bites that we hear throughout the day from radio, print and TV media, Internet sources, social media, and everyday human interaction is not the way to form opinions that guide our life decisions. Unfortunately and most concerning is that too often we do!

Those who present news and refer to themselves as journalists should be presenting news to inform, not opinions to influence, right? Well, sometimes.

At the time of writing this book, we have seen one major news anchor suspended and then permanently replaced for not reporting factually and embellishing his personal experiences relating to news accounts. And a second anchor, referred to as a network's chief political journalist, apologized for his lack of transparency regarding past and present political figures he had once worked for.

These are supposedly trusted national news journalists—or are they? Remember the question: are these so-called journalists more interested in personal ambitions and agendas, or are they truly concerned with factual, unbiased news accounts? Please ask yourselves this and carefully evaluate your conclusion.

I believe we should have our eyes wide open and demand that that those who present the news do so in a factual, fair, and balanced manner.

What would be the result if a news organization purposely held back certain known facts from an important news story?

Would this be an example of silent thought? Yes, most definitely. So you can see how easily this could be the case. Think about how damaging and counterproductive this intentional action can be if done by our major news outlets.

I believe that many people mistake opinions for factual news, which can easily happen if so-called unbiased news reports are really rooted in the opinions of the presenter.

Remember—we are discussing this in the context of spontaneous thought. How do we combat this and not repeat these sound bites to others we encounter, perpetuating misinformation and furthering a false narrative?

In fairness, depending on the topic, this may not be concerning. But if this is a topic with significant importance to the American way of life, our lives and those closest to us, we must rethink our approach to this tendency and find ways to counteract it.

Should we be more discerning when we choose our news outlets? Yes, without question!

Should we choose to hear different views on major topics to better inform ourselves before choosing a position? Yes, most definitely!

One of my greatest concerns is that with the many challenges in our daily lives, we sometimes block out the most important issues affecting our way of life. If we rely only on spontaneous thought, we could be yielding the freedoms that allow us to choose independent thought and expression.

Ask yourself, are we more concerned with a news story about Bruce Jenner becoming Caitlin Jenner than politics on the local and national level that have dramatic effects on the American way of life? Unfortunately, in many cases we focus more on the notoriety of a Jenner story than politics.

Let's think about the print media, such as our major city newspapers. Ask yourself why you read a newspaper. Is it for national news, sports, finance, the local sports and news, or just the lighter side pages, such as travel and trends or the comics? Perhaps you are more interested in the editorial and op-ed pages.

Have you ever heard the phrase *above and below the fold*, which intends to highlight the major news story or stories of the day? In most cases, front-page stories present an introduction to a story of varying length, followed by a notation to find the remaining story on a page within the newspaper.

Is this done for a particular reason? Is it possible that the paper wants you to page through additional pages, possibly stopping as other story lines or advertisements catch your attention? Perhaps.

By the way, when reading my Sunday paper, I do page through, and there it is every week, that same Rolex watch ad, and I think, *Well, maybe someday,* and then continue to the next page.

I do not have an issue with this practice or any other in order to market a product. The print media has faced a great deal of competition with the onset of the Internet, and you will find many people reading tablets or other handheld devices instead of a traditional newspaper.

Why choose a newspaper when you already have access to the Internet and in most cases would have to purchase the newspaper? Possibly we prefer newspapers because we do not want to surf the net, and a particular paper has the diversity to satisfy our need for information or creates a different comfort level.

However, what I do have a problem with is this: if within these so-called major news stories, the writer tries to construct the story in a way to influence the reader with personal agendas rather than simply stating the factual account of the story. If true, ask yourself, should this paper not confine these opinions to its editorial page or op-ed pages?

But let's get back to the spontaneous thought. How does what I just described affect our thought process? Certainly, when we decide to pick up a newspaper or magazine, we intend to spend more time on thought than just causal interaction. Here, spontaneous thought occurs if we read a news account of importance and form an opinion without applying any validation of the story's accuracy.

This is also an example of silent thought, meaning we do not take the time to apply additional thought to validate accuracy.

Please bear in mind that I am not suggesting that we painstakingly take these steps with every topic and thought we encounter. As I described earlier, we have many thoughts that are not significant. I am speaking of the major aspects of our lives and how the actions of others can have a great effect on our way of life.

I strongly encourage spontaneous thought; think of all the great improvements to our quality of life that would not exist if thoughts were not articulated or acted on, resulting in a wide variety of positive changes in our daily lives.

Many of these certainly started as a spontaneous thought and, if not acted upon, would have fallen into the silent thought chamber of our brain, possibly never to be heard of again.

Conversely, examine how incorrect thought has had adverse effects on human lives.

Remember: one of my reasons for writing this book is rooted in my determination to understand what promotes thought or the lack of thought altogether—and then understand why thought does not progress to expression in either word or action.

I would also like to emphasize that we can relate spontaneous and silent thought to all aspects of our lives. However, I am greatly concerned with how our American political system exploits silent thought and will concentrate on that concept.

Silent thought can be found in everyone, irrespective of who you are, employed or unemployed, at all income levels, those highly educated and those less educated. There will be varying degrees of silent thought due to these factors.

Ask yourself, do I really need to spend my valuable time or even my idle time thinking about politics? Does politics, national as well as local, really affect every aspect of my life? Yes to both, without question. Both directly and indirectly.

With greater awareness, we can proceed to look at what we should do about it. If we never experience thought on national or more global issues, we may be yielding our right to participate in the future of our country. Worst of all, we may be allowing those in politics and those in the media who promote their own agendas to influence our thoughts.

Is this an example of identity theft? Yes—ours! Please think about this and honestly evaluate the validity of this thought. You may be very surprised at the results.

# Chapter 2

## TARGETED THOUGHT

Targeted thought can happen in two primary ways, either initiated by us or by others!

First, it happens when we take the initiative to choose a topic and study it, usually with some degree of research. Hopefully, this is a subject of importance (it usually is), but what prompts this action?

Is it due to personal decisions needed or workplace decisions that require our focus? Yes to both. Each and every day, we are constantly changing our thought priorities as we develop from infancy through adulthood. So along this path, our targeted thoughts will change.

Let's think more in terms of our targeted thought relating to personal decisions. I think of these in two categories: first, those that govern our values, moral consciousness, and character, and then second, those that we choose for entertainment, which can be found in so many different ways.

I do not believe it is necessary for us to cover workplace decisions here, as there are so many. However, I will stress that in our workplace decisions, we should still apply targeted thought with respect to how those decisions can affect the other aspects of our daily lives. Please do not leave any thoughts relating to work in that silent thought chamber of your brain.

Now, with respect to targeted thought on personal decisions, let's concern ourselves with the first category mentioned above that develops and governs our values, moral consciousness, and character. For now, let's leave to the side the second category relating to our choices for entertainment.

What do you attribute your personal development to? What and who has influenced your beliefs?

Have you emulated a person or persons in your family, or a circle of friends, or have you chosen a figure by name and stature to emulate?

How much time do you spend thinking about these traits and values?

What is in your personal toolkit—strengths, weaknesses, achievements, successes, failures?

These are all very good questions to ask, and not just once in a lifetime. We should challenge ourselves to assess our character traits, values, and morality as many times as necessary throughout our lives.

Once you do this, it is extremely important to find balance in the flow of information you allow to enter the brain. Don't allow just one source to dictate or trigger thought and your analysis. We should be objective and open-minded when forming our character and beliefs.

Let's hope that our foundations are strong, meaning we have received a great deal of influence from our parents and those who have guided us during our childhood to adulthood, allowing us to build on a strong footing.

This is not to say that every one of us has been fortunate enough to have a guiding hand in our childhood development. Do not worry. If you are thinking about this honestly and believe in yourself, you can and will find a path to build your character.

Have you ever thought about why you are the way you are? Are you unsure about what has impacted your character traits, beliefs, and values, yet at the same time you know you possess these characteristics that cause the actions you take in life?

This may be a result of silent thought—meaning, over a period of time, you have subjected yourself, as we all do, to the many facets of life, opinions and actions of others, so that now your beliefs and opinions are greatly influenced by others and are not a result of your own thoughtful analysis.

I am always amazed at how uninformed or misinformed some of us are with respect to our American political system, given the access that most Americans have to the Internet.

This is a tremendous source for multiple sources of information, in order to guide our thought processes and not be limited or subjected to the targeted influences of others. Even if you do not have access to the Internet, there is always the public library.

Today's Internet search engines provide us with an incredible opportunity to quickly seek out information, along with many differing views.

Yet we do not to spend any significant amount of time on our country's politics and politicians, which have a great deal of influence on our freedoms to make our personal life choices. Why?      Well, part of the reason is what we discussed earlier. We just don't think it is worth our time, and we have not connected the dots in the way that would allow us to see the impact on our lives, and instead we would rather embrace the more enjoyable aspects of life.

After all, we have lives filled with many challenges and obligations, so how can we possibly take the time to worry about politics? Politicians know this and exploit this. Don't give up. There is a solution, so please keep reading!

The second primary way targeted thought can occur is when actions are initiated by other parties that specifically attempt to influence our thoughts and then influence our actions and beliefs.

Now, I do want to mention that this can be just fine and is something that many of us welcome, as we want to be presented with stimuli and enjoy our daily consumption of all sorts of information.

Others are more guarded and limit the intake from unsolicited sources, deciding to search out information and clarity on topics by initiating targeted thought, as described earlier in this chapter.

Targeted thought will come at us in many ways, written and spoken via many conduits—radio, television, print sources such as newspapers and magazines, the Internet, blogs, social sites, and more. Just think of all the ways you encounter information throughout your day; it's almost dizzying.

For example, think about all the advertisements embedded in your favorite newspaper, magazine, or website. You may be simply reading a news account or searching out an answer, and there they are, the graphics, popups, banners, or whatever, to redirect your attention to an ad.

Ask yourself, why don't these sources just place all these ads in one section? Is it because they do not want it to be your choice to check out an advertisement? Of course it is!

We live in the greatest country in the world, with a vibrant capitalistic economy. So we should enjoy and take advantage of free competition for all to participate in either as a seller or buyer of goods, services, and information.

Certainly, we should be discerning and objective in how we let these influences affect our actions.

Let's now think about those who intentionally target our thoughts and take initiatives to not only influence our thought but also modify our political and social beliefs.

What would the outcome be if this was done in an insidious way, with the express desire to modify our thinking and not for any other reason? Let's look closer at the meaning of the word *insidious* as Webster's dictionary defines it: awaiting a chance to entrap; treacherous, harmful but enticing, having a gradual and cumulative effect.

Carefully review that definition and ask yourself, are our politicians, political pundits (those who think they know what is in the best interest for America), and those in the news media with personal ambitions and political agendas capable of engaging in this behavior? Yes, without question!

Not every politician or those affiliated with the political process engage in this deception, but many do. It is also fair to say that not all of those in the media act this way, but again, many do.

The most disturbing part of this is that the so-called news journalists in this country should be an objective filter between those in politics and us, the American public. Additionally, these journalists must vet every politician in the same way, irrespective of party affiliation.

The next time you watch or hear a press interview with a politician or political strategist, take particular notice of the context of the question.

Is it a well-constructed inquiry to an important topic that would challenge the responding party to answer succinctly and honestly, or is it simply a question that only allows the responding party to respond with platitudes, vagueness, and no relevance to the question asked?

Watch different news programs and honestly compare the competence of the interviewer and the seriousness of his or her questions. Please include a source that you typically do not watch or listen to—not opinion talk shows but so-called news programs.

One revealing indicator to notice is, after the responding party does not answer the question, even though he or she just spoke for several minutes, does the interviewer restate or press for an answer to the question or just accept a nonanswer and move on to the next question to be avoided?

Ask yourself, is the interviewer just making an appearance of asking a probing question with no real interest in a relevant response? Yes, in many cases.

Ask yourself, why would a so-called serious news journalist with many years of experience allow distortion of factual news in this way?

Is this not just an example of a journalist using his or her forum to further a politician or political party's agenda, which means he or she has the same agenda? Sure it is!

Is this news? Of course not. It is a deliberate attempt to target our thought process with agendas to alter our beliefs. They disguise this process as news and not opinion, because if they did identify it as opinion and not news, very few of us would accept them as credible unbiased news outlets.

Some of us will quickly see this and will discredit it. Unfortunately, many of us accept this encounter as factual news and repeat the falsehood many times. Again, silent thought occurs. We should not allow spontaneous thought to misguide us, which is what they are hoping for.

The press should not act as a conduit between a politician or political party and the American public by taking a politician or party's agenda and reporting that as factual news. They should not pick and choose in this way. If they do, we should immediately remove them from our chosen news sources.

If we want opinion, we can easily find that, but when it comes to presenting the critical news accounts of the day, we have to demand facts—and only the facts. It is a waste of our valuable time to do otherwise, and we should accept nothing less.

Believe me, once these institutions and those who practice this realize that we now understand these tactics, they will change or become irrelevant.

Remember this: those who engage in this malpractice have refined this greatly and disguise their behavior very well. They take the long view, the same way for example that advertisers do, meaning they will constantly target your thought process in order to eventually convince you to adopt their beliefs and values.

This may be okay when deciding to buy a car, home, clothes, or the many other life choices we undertake. But choosing whom to vote for or taking a misinformed position based on tainted facts can lead to a serious erosion of every freedom we cherish.

Remember my earlier comment about identity theft. Please do not let this happen to you!

I do want to mention that television and radio opinion talk shows of a political nature can be very valuable. Why? Hearing different points of view is an important step in keeping an open mind.

They also can stimulate our thinking in different ways, depending on who is engaging in the debate. It can help you to allow the subject of politics to take up more of your consciousness.

I encourage you not to simply listen to shows that only have hosts and guests of the same opinion; this is boring and counterproductive. Choose programs that offer point and counterpoint formats and that have guests with different political opinions and beliefs. You will find this much more stimulating to your thought process.

Those who offer only one belief and ridicule those with differing views don't want intellectual debates, and you will find these are the same people trying to target your thoughts, which is okay, as long as you realize this is happening.

If you decide to listen to an opinion talk show, you expect to hear opinions, which everyone is entitled to and is a true expression of our freedoms.

In the last two chapters, we have discussed both spontaneous and targeted thought, along with how and why silent thought occurs.

In the following chapters, I hope to further explain how politics is interwoven into every American's life. We will discuss several crises currently facing America. I hope my readers gain a better understanding of when and how silent thought interconnects with these major crises of our day.

In the final chapter, we will discuss how all of the crises are interconnected, and we will discuss solutions to combat silent thought.

# Chapter 3

# AMERICAN CRISIS NUMBER ONE
# LEADERSHIP IN AMERICA

Whom do you look to for leadership? Many people might say God, parents, a sibling, a teacher, or a coach.

How many times have we changed our minds about whom we choose as a leader? How many times have we been disappointed in our leaders? I would like to think that we will change as many times as necessary, but ask yourself, what makes an effective leader?

Have you ever noticed that those who proclaim to be a leader are not really leading but are trying to advocate a personal belief that may or not be in the best interest of the people that follow him or her?

Have you ever thought about the *perception principle*? This principle identifies three views: first, how you perceive yourself; second, how you think others perceive you, and; third, how others actually do perceive you.

The answers could be very different among all three, and the third might really surprise many of us.

If we do not lead, what is our role? Are we simply just followers? Yes, there a many of us who just follow the lead of others. Certainly there are many of us who are leaders with respect to our own lives and those of our children. But outside of the family unit, are we taking any leadership roles?

Sure we do, in all walks of life, both in our workplaces and in our places of worship. I would like to point out—some may agree and others not—that the exception to those leaders that might fail us is God, who is infallible. This book is not written from this perspective, but it is an important distinction to mention.

I would like to see America become a nation of leaders, with all of its citizens in leadership roles, taking responsibility for their own lives and holding those in politics accountable for their actions. Have you ever heard the saying "take an ownership mentality"? Think about it.

Unfortunately, many citizens allow silent thought to restrict their ability to lead in this way. Our strength as a nation resides in our citizens, not in a few politicians in Washington, DC. So please do not ever yield your leadership role!

Now, let's think about leadership in more depth regarding our politicians, both in local and national offices. Politicians often forget that we elect them to take the lead on issues and follow a direction we believe to be in our best interest, not try to lead us in a direction of policy that they believe is in our best interest.

This is one of the reasons we are so disappointed in many of our so-called political leaders. This is also why we must focus and think more about this crisis at this time.

I am going to focus the rest of this chapter on leaders that hold national office rather than try to look at local politicians. However, the same deficiencies exist at your local level as well.

Considering the focus of this book, let's look at the top six leaders in our government: the president, vice president, speaker of the house, Senate majority leader, House minority leader, Senate minority leader.

First, our president.

During the 2008 Democrat presidential primary, I enthusiastically supported Barack Obama. I did so for two very important reasons in my view.

His chief rival was Hillary Clinton, who in my analysis was not the right choice for our nation. I felt it would be more politics as usual, the same old lip service, and I was uncomfortable with many of her core beliefs.

Additionally, I just did not find her trustworthy and felt her to be too partisan. Too many instances of her embellishing her life experiences, too much of a politician. I simply did not see her as an inclusive leader and possessing true leadership qualities.

As of the writing of this book, Mrs. Clinton has again entered the race for the Democrat nomination in 2016 and likely will be her party's nominee. My concerns from 2008 have only grown stronger. Further thoughts on this in a later chapter.

Now my first reason for supporting Mr. Obama. I felt he presented a reasonable possibility for change for the better in our broken political system—that simple. I was optimistic that he could accomplish his stated goals for change in American politics.

Sure, I listened very closely to all the arguments against his candidacy—inexperience, too new to national politics, and many more—but felt he could overcome these challenges if he would truly put the interest of all Americans over those entrenched political interests in Washington, DC.

As the primary season ended and as we moved through the general election, I was delighted to see the country's excitement level continue to rise at the prospect of him winning the presidency.

I believe this was for many reasons, including the prospect that our country would see positive change in how our government conducted itself, the enthusiasm that change was possible, and certainly, not the least of reasons, was that America would elect its first black president.

After the election, I felt it important to monitor President Obama's actions and words. For the first several months, I watched and listened to the daily White House press briefings and whatever presidential orders or statements were issued, as well as the president's approach to naming his cabinet.

I found that whitehouse.gov and CSPAN were very helpful in providing access to these daily events. Doing this was challenging, due to all of my other commitments, but I felt this necessary to determine whether my thought process was correct in voting for Mr. Obama.

I was also very anxious to see tangible change and if campaign promises were kept or if they just found their way out the president's consciousness.

As the president's first year in office progressed, I started to notice a more rigid ideology take hold. Having strong core beliefs is certainly part of effective leadership, but rigid ideology without the willingness for debate is counterproductive and not in America's best interest.

During his first two years in office, President Obama's party controlled both the US House of Representatives and the US Senate. The speaker of the House was Nancy Pelosi, and the Senate majority leader was Harry Reid. These two individuals also demonstrated strong tendencies toward rigid ideology and were very partisan.

The narrative by many, not all, in the political sphere that started to develop was that if one were to disagree with or criticize the president, his or her motive, if white, must be racially motivated.

Of course, this was simply ridiculous and used only as a distraction instead of engaging in an honest exchange of ideas and debate on the issue in question. This was just the beginning of the divisive politics that now consume Washington, DC.

The reason for mentioning this is that we can see how silent thought is employed by those who wish to distract and shut down debate.

The racial nature of this narrative also creates silent thought among many Americans, who decide not to participate in the discussion with dissenting views, for fear of being labeled a racist.

Is any of this leadership? Of course not!

Presidential leadership is rooted in the office of the president, not in the person holding that office. The person coming into the office brings leadership qualities that either enhance the presidency or diminish it.

A key quality that must exist in presidential leadership is the ability to inspire greatness in each and every citizen, not just the ones that support your views and cast their ballot in your favor.

The presidency is not about the greatness of one man or one woman; it is the greatness of America as a unified, thriving nation that leads the world in every aspect of human achievement.

So why would any politician practice politics to divide rather than unite? Well, unfortunately the answer is that they are pursuing personal ambitions rather than American greatness.

Do you remember our discussion in the last chapter regarding insidious motives? Ask yourself, does this behavior meet that definition?

Sadly, I believe that President Obama is practicing divisive politics, meaning he sees the need to divide America along the lines of race, gender, and age, wealthy, poor, and political ideology.

In doing this, he is distracting us from the vital need to solve the serious challenges we face as a nation. This is not what he promised during his campaign!

He is not the only politician practicing this. Many, irrespective of party affiliation, are practicing these same destructive tactics, along with some in the media and some inside of our political institutions.

I know some of my readers will push back on this assertion, and I respect that. I ask you to fairly evaluate where we are in 2016 in the eighth year of the Obama presidency.

Please do not rely on all the targeted sound bites you have heard during his presidency and that have secured their place in your consciousness. Rather, resist the silent thought tendency and challenge yourself to truly evaluate his leadership.

Please ask yourself the following:

- Is our current president more concerned with personal ambition and legacy than anything else?

- Does he spend more time applauding America's greatness or more time apologizing for or criticizing America?

- Does he project humility in the office he holds or does he project arrogance and a sense of being more important than that same office?

- Has he completely politicized every major issue facing our nation?

Please search out the answers to these questions with your critical thought and analysis and not by just accepting the opinions of others.

I am not comfortable in criticizing our president because of the great respect that I have for the office of the presidency and our country, but I feel it absolutely vital that we insist that the person who holds the presidency be held accountable and truly be an inspirational leader for all Americans.

Another very important leadership quality to have as president is the ability to ensure those you appoint to major cabinet posts are delivering their respective agency services fairly and then to hold them accountable when they don't perform their responsibilities in the best interest of the American people.

Let's look at two agencies. The first is the IRS. This agency not only spent millions of dollars on wasteful, so-called work-related seminars or retreats that were laughable and unnecessary but was also allowed to target tax-exempt groups for their political beliefs and to restrict their views and freedoms.

The second example is the Veterans Administration hospitals across this country, where it was discovered that our vets were waiting months for care, received inadequate care or no care at all, and in many cases were treated as faceless numbers rather than the heroes they are.

Some of our vets that survived the battlefield tragically lost their lives while waiting for the proper care they so justly deserved from these VA hospitals!

This VA hospital example is still a serious problem at the time of writing this book, after more than a year since the problem was first discovered. Search out the number of our vets committing suicide each day. You will be shocked!

When the president was asked when he was made aware of these issues, his response was that he heard about them like every other American, through news accounts.

Ask yourself, being completely honest in your thought process, is this leadership? Absolutely not!

Also, look at the distractions presented by the media and others in trying to deflect blame regarding these two examples. This is another display of how targeted thought is used to manipulate our thoughts through meaningless sound bites in the hope that the American public will accept the excuses and move on.

Please do not ever accept the excuse from any politician or any defender of the status quo that a government agency is very complicated, and therefore solutions are difficult, and the American public must be more patient or more understanding.

This could not be further from the truth. One of the reasons these breakdowns (some refer to as scandals) in government occur is because government is too large, which creates an unaccountable bureaucracy and workforce.

It has been truly disheartening to see President Obama act in this way. I had very high expectations for him when he took office. Could he make a course correction?

To change, he would have to accept the fact that the office he holds is not about him or his legacy but rather the future of the American people, and he is there to safeguard that future, not further his own political and personal ambitions!

Unfortunately, I do not think he has the humility or the capacity to think of it in this way and is consumed with his rigid ideology. He has his own opinions, and we should respect that. However, he is gravely wrong—no bias, just strong disagreement.

I can respect his policy views and those who agree, but I cannot agree with the tactic of divisive politics, which accomplishes only further division and strife in our country.

Let's look at two former presidents, John Kennedy and Ronald Reagan, and two quotes from each.

First from John Kennedy, "Ask not what your country can do for you, ask what you can do for your country."

Second from Ronald Reagan, "Peace through strength."

These comments were made in similar contexts and were made more than twenty years apart. These two presidents had great leadership qualities and understood that the greatness of America and a united citizenry are far more important than a single person occupying the White House.

One of the most important responsibilities of the presidency is to protect our nation from all foreign enemies that seek to destroy America and those that wish to kill Americans either here or around the world.

Many have said, and I strongly agree, "That those who seek to harm America, should so fear us that they would never want to meet us on the battlefield, but rather instead choose to sit across from us at the negotiating table."

The way we accomplish this and ensure the freedoms that we cherish is to have a military second to none. Our military should be stronger than that of any other two or three countries' militaries combined that are closest to our military's capacity and who currently threaten the world.

I know that some will challenge this, but those who do ignore not only world history but American history and how America has defeated evil time and time again.

I will, however, stress that our military needs reform, not reduction!

It has to possess the highest levels of technology, tactical weaponry, and strategic dominance along with the best and brightest personnel. So when I say stronger, I don't mean just simply more personnel.

The reform I am speaking about is dealing with the wasteful spending that has crept into our military structure, as it has in many of our other government agencies. Our military budget requires a large percentage of our tax dollars, and the military has to be held accountable for every dollar it spends.

This is where others are wrong, thinking that just cutting our military budget and/or the number of personnel is the answer. And yes, our politicians politicize our military, and that has to stop!

Our military's leaders, along with its civilian counterparts, must always look several years ahead and plan accordingly. How in the world did we ever allow ISIS to reach its deadly prominence?

Who failed America here? Our president or our military?

Our current president does not understand or chooses not to accept the reality of what a country's military provides its citizens.

Our nation cannot continue to thrive without the assurances of a military that ensures our protection and our ability to practice the liberty and freedoms that have created America's greatness, which is the envy of the world!

President Obama chooses to reduce our military and marginalizes it in his efforts to marginalize the United States as just another nation in a world of many and to diminish our standing as a superpower.

This could not be more dangerous to America and the world!

JFK and Ronald Reagan understood the importance of our military's strength and how and when to use it.

The US president is often referred to as the "leader of the free world" by many around the world. The key word here is *leader.* If this person is not an effective leader, the consequences can be disastrous not only for America but for the entire free world.

I ask you, is our president behaving as the leader of the free world?

Here again, it is important to remember that the person holding the office of president is not the force that the world is looking to, but rather America is the force for leadership in the world.

Therefore, if our president projects strength, then America will appear strong, and conversely, if our president projects weakness, America will appear weak and will be challenged over and over again, both militarily and strategically.

President Obama is currently negotiating with Iran over their ambitions to develop and deliver a nuclear weapon. This is just the most recent example of President Obama's weakness as a leader.

Why do I say this? Well, let's consider some very important aspects.

When entering these negotiations, America possessed a very powerful position. Unified sanctions with other nations against Iran were in place, which is really what brought Iran to the negotiating table in the first place—Iran's economy in turmoil, along with fear of military strikes by Israel or the United States.

So what do our president and the current secretary of state, another weak leader, do? They yielded to Iran's demands and, by doing so, weakened our position of strength.

They also agreed to more and more extensions to find a way to make a deal. Why would they do this?

Instead of showing weakness by granting extensions, why did they not just suspend negotiations?

Why did the president not let Iran see that he might agree with Congress and toughen the sanctions?

Did they not enter these talks with a clear vision of what was at stake and what would be the nonnegotiable concessions that Iran would have to make?

Why would our president act is if we were negotiating a deal with a friendly country or ally, rather than dealing with the seriousness of an enemy trying to develop a nuclear weapon and a country that would likely use it or allow one of its proxies to use it?

Are we not adept enough to understand Iran for who they really are, a state sponsor of terrorism and a country where its leader and people continually shout, "Death to America and Israel"?

Has Iran not participated in or been a party to the death of American soldiers in Iraq?

Do we not believe that Iran seeks to establish its dominance in the region, as other nations in that region, including Israel, have warned about many times over?

Please do not be fooled or misguided by those trying to make this deal or those who support it when they are questioned about how this is being handled and respond that these negotiations are very delicate and complicated and the American people should be patient. Really!

There is nothing complicated about these negotiations!

Sure, some diplomatic negotiations between nations can be very difficult and require concessions on both sides. This is not one.

However, those on our side of the table are making it more complicated and very doubtful for an acceptable American result when they continually extend deadlines, yield to Iran's demands, and treat this as if they were negotiating with a trustworthy nation.

We have all the leverage, yet we are behaving in a timid and weak manner, as if Iran held leverage over us and its neighbors.

How incompetent is it of our president and secretary of state not to recognize this? Ask yourself, why are we even discussing lifting sanctions until Iran signs an unconditional agreement to stop and dismantle its nuclear program?

Then they must demonstrate that they are adhering to the agreement, including unchallenged inspections. Then and only then should we start to phase in any relief in sanctions.

One of the reasons Russia and China want an agreement and the arms embargo lifted is so that they can sell weapons and weapon systems to Iran.

Does this stabilize this region or further destabilize the region? Is the answer not obvious?

Do you really believe that it would be easy to snap back the sanctions, as our president insists, if Iran failures to honor an agreement? The naïve behavior of those negotiating for America is stunning.

The other tactic they employ is that of using a straw man argument, such as if we do not find a deal, then what is the other alternative? War?

You see, when they use the word *war*, they intend to frighten Americans over that prospect and silence those who disagree.

They are attempting to remove the American citizen from the decision process and convince us that we could not possibly understand this diplomatic effort and/or label those who disagree as warmongers.

Americans are much smarter than to be fooled by these distractions or illusions and must not allow those who are disingenuous on this subject to target our thoughts in this way.

This president seeks to have his way and only his way by distorting the facts when speaking to the American public.

Some have said the reason for all of this illogical behavior by the president and secretary of state is desperation for any deal to enhance their respective legacies.

Is it another example of our president politicizing a critical issue, one of national security, rather taking a straightforward America-first approach?

It is very concerning to see America embarrassed by their incompetence, which only gives Iran and the rest of the world the impression that a signed deal is more important than all the perils of Iran securing a nuclear weapon and the means to deliver it with an intercontinental ballistic missile.

Now that a deal has been agreed to, what does our president do?

He sends this agreement to the United Nations Security Council to be voted on before even sending it to Congress, so that America, through its elected representatives, has an opportunity to review and either vote to approve or disapprove.

Why would President Obama not put America first, instead of looking to the UN first?

Well first, again on display is his arrogance, where he thinks his view should be accepted without question. Second, he believes that UN approval will give this deal more influence over the US Congress.

Again, he is trying to manipulate America's thought through the appearance that it must be a good deal if the UN approves of it.

Ask yourself, why did we not insist on the four Americans being held by Iran to be released as part of this agreement?

The president and secretary of state have both made conflicting comments on why this was not considered or accomplished.

Not ensuring their release further highlights to the world the incompetence and weakness of these leaders and their failure to negotiate from a position of strength.

This was made part of the conversation only after the president was embarrassed by a question during a press conference.

Before commencing any negotiations with Iran, the preconditions at the very least should have been the release of these Americans, retractions by Iran's leaders of "death to America," and for Iran's leaders to acknowledge the right of Israel to exist as a nation!

These are not complicated concepts, but our current leaders choose to serve their personal ambitions rather than serve the American people.

At no other time have the countries in the Middle East, including Saudi Arabia, Egypt, Jordan, and Turkey as well as Israel, been more ready to form a coalition against Iran, waiting for America to take the lead.

So what does our president do? He hesitates, leads from behind, ignores some of these country's leaders, and allows more and more destabilization to occur in the region, along with deadly consequences.

He has taken the same approach when dealing with ISIS.

Our foreign policy under this president continues to falter and lacks any strategic thought for America's interest.

Please consider Russia and China, as well as the Middle East. Are these countries creating more or less stability in the world?

This president is attempting to construct his legacy at the peril of America and the free world.

I want to be clear. I do not have any issue with a president that is concerned with his or her legacy while in office, especially when considering the high office of the presidency and the oath of office he or she takes.

What this president and others that have held this office fail to realize is a president that governs with only the American people's best interests in mind and not with his or her own personal interests and ambitions shaping their decisions will have no problem with legacy and will rank very high in our presidential history.

So again, ask yourself, being impartial, is this the type of leadership we should accept?

Would JFK or Ronald Reagan have led in this way?

I would like to cite another example of the lack of national leadership, and then we must move on to other chapters.

Our president's resistance to approve the Keystone Pipeline and open government land for lease for oil and natural gas exploration further weakens our nation.

Think all of the years that we have been told by our political leaders that we need to engage the Middle East due to our dependence on oil and how that region's politics affect our nation and our foreign policy decisions.

Now, our nation, through its technology advances, has created an energy boom in natural gas and oil production. We are on the threshold of becoming the world's leader in oil production and currently lead in natural gas production.

Look at the benefits for America as a result—very low and sustainable gas prices, which has created more disposable income for every American, not to mention how lower energy costs have had positive benefits for other sectors of our economy, which enables growth and prosperity.

Our nation's oil production has also helped to lower oil prices on the world market, which also creates financial stress on some exporting countries that don't share our same values and worldviews, due to the high cost of extracting their oil.

Sure, American companies are experiencing the same issue, but with our technology and innovation, they will continue to reduce their cost of extraction and rise above these challenges. That's America!

So why does our president resist this incredible opportunity for energy independence? Is he again politically motivated and simply conceding to his political base, or is it again his rigid ideology that prevents him from taking proactive steps to embrace this American opportunity?

Yes to both questions!

Think about the benefits that having the world's strongest military along with being the world's energy leader could afford to all Americans. Not even considering a stronger economy, these are all national security imperatives.

Do you remember in the campaign leading up to the 2008 and 2012 elections, where President Obama's opponents spoke to energy independence, and how Mr. Obama and his supporters ridiculed these opponents over these positions?

Do you remember his recurring comments that "you cannot drill your way out this problem," and "we should get used to the reality of higher gas prices."

Really!

How can one president be so wrong on so many issues?

We have a crisis of political leadership in this country, especially with respect the six national figures I cited at the beginning of this chapter, not just the president and secretary of state.

I will spend more time on the other political leaders I mentioned earlier in a later chapter.

I am not trying to impugn the president's character, and I want to stress that I do not get any pleasure in criticizing President Obama while in office.

However, I and every other American have the right to question and disagree with his actions and motives. And yes, criticize all of our elected officials when we feel that they are not acting in the best interest of all Americans!

So please do not yield your right to free speech and succumb to others and their attempts to influence your thought process, and please do not succumb to silent thought on your part, assuming our nation's leadership is not in crisis and does not deserve your full attention.

# Chapter 4

# AMERICAN CRISIS NUMBER TWO
# POLITICAL CORRECTNESS

What is political correctness, also referred to as "PC"?

Let's start with how dictionary.com defines it:

- Marked by or adhering to a typical progressive orthodoxy on issues involving especially ethnicity, gender, sexual orientations, or ecology.

- Demonstrating progressive ideals, avoiding vocabulary that is considered offensive, discriminatory, or judgmental, esp. concerning race and gender.

Why are we concerned with this as Americans? Or are we?

If this is progressive, are we moving forward or are we falling backward?

We have a political party in this country that self-identifies as progressives or progressive liberals, so does this represent all of America? Certainly not, unless you are part of this group.

So again, ask yourself, why are we concerned as Americans with political correctness? I believe we should be more concerned with "American correctness" and not just a set of subjective ideals promoted by a particular political party and those who may agree with it.

Is this not just another example of an individual or group of people trying to influence others who don't agree with them?

Sure it is, and it is also a serious attempt to target America's consciousness in a controlled way, with no room for debate, just strict adherence to their beliefs.

One of the reasons this is taking root in America is that, as discussed earlier, we have a media that in large part promotes this political party's agenda over others. This comes at us as targeted sound bites that root themselves in the minds of many Americans, without any validation.

Why? Well again, remember the silent thought tendency to just accept thought inspired by others without challenging the validity, whether or not it is accurate, and if it is just the biased views of others, meaning, it is just their opinion.

Have you noticed lately, that more and more of these people who practice this deceit will say that not following their political correctness ideals goes against who we are as Americans. This is an attempt to shut down your analysis of their viewpoints and simply accept and follow their logic.

Another tactic to accomplish their goal is to portray those who disagree as racist, sexist, biased or bigoted, unintelligent or simply not as smart as they are, and not worthy of their respect. These are elitist views and do not depict American correctness.

Do not be fooled or misled by these tactics. We do not need a narrow viewpoint for how we should speak and live as Americans, or for any one group insisting that all of America should subscribe to their views.

The difference between *American correctness* and *political correctness* is that American correctness does not restrict Americans in what they think or say, does not try to limit our freedoms, and seeks to preserve America's history, values, and traditions.

Have you ever watched one of these people that promote political correctness try to explain his or her narrow viewpoint or agenda? They almost, literally, contort themselves before your eyes with all of this distraction and distortion. Watch this closely!

Americans will treat other Americans correctly without the need for these narrow viewpoints or twisted values. American values have always been and will continue to be the guiding principles for America.

Sure, there are some in America who choose to hate and injure others, both in word and action, but we have laws in place to deal with this when appropriate.

We do not need political correctness disguised as a solution to combat this, when in reality this is nothing more than a small group of people, unfortunately with national media influence, attempting to shut down debate or compromise to find an American solution, preferring that we just follow their twisted viewpoint on how Americans should act.

An example of the incorrectness of political correctness at the time of writing this book is the controversy over the flying of the confederate flag on the state's capital grounds after the senseless murder of nine black Americans in a church prayer meeting in Charleston, South Carolina.

A young man and a racist filled with hate murdered these nine innocents as he sat among them.

In the days that followed this horrific act, a photo was discovered of the killer holding a confederate flag.

Immediately after, many started calling for the removal of the flag from the capital grounds, followed by knee-jerk reactions, such as calls to remove the flag from appearing in other southern states' flags, removing it from license plates, and removing a 1970s television show that featured a car with this flag on its roof.

And of course, our president weighed in, using this tragedy to speak about gun control. Sure, in his remarks, he also condemned the act and spoke to the loss for family and friends of the victims.

But ask yourself, was his effort only to disguise his remarks and only speak to his true motive, to again politicize a tragedy and promote his views on gun control? Think about it!

Now we know that killer's background check when purchasing the gun was handled incorrectly with respect to his criminal background investigation. If handled properly, he would not have been allowed to purchase a gun.

So again, we have a tragedy and senseless loss of life, and the real issues surrounding the case are ignored!

Why are we not focusing on why this young man's behavior and signs of hate and disorder were not acted on instead of this flag distraction or more gun control laws that did not cause this heinous act?

Of course, those that use this tragedy to divert America's attention will never speak to this, because that discussion does not fit into their narrative and narrow set of viewpoints.

An encouraging example of American correctness after this tragedy was how the citizens of Charleston, black and white alike, came together in prayer and unity, without riots or violent protests.

I heard a news interview conducted with Andrew Young, the former mayor of Atlanta, Georgia, and civil rights leader who marched alongside Dr. Martin Luther King Jr.

Mr. Young remarked, "Taking down the flag doesn't solve anything and had nothing to do with this act." He went on to say, "We should not wipe out our past but rather find ways to live together in the future."

He also commented that he would not trade one job for this flag. You see, Mr. Young is a leader who can reflect on our past injustices and at the same time choose to look forward to all Americans living together.

While this flag is not a great example of unity for America, it is, however, a part of America's history and has different meanings for different people, people who don't have hate in their hearts for other Americans. Their views are just as important as anyone else's.

Have you noticed that many of these people calling for political correctness are politicians? Ask yourself, are these politicians more concerned with the real issues at hand or their own political futures? We will discuss this in more detail in a later chapter.

Political correctness at its roots is a tactic to control freedom of speech, disguised as an enlightened way of thought. It is really only a way to promote silent thought!

Let's continue to analyze this.

I have always thought about why we feel the need to hyphenate certain race or ethnicities for some Americans. For example, when speaking of black Americans, we see those who practice PC use *African-American* at least once and then use *black American* in their remaining comments.

Why do we do this? I am of Italian, Irish, and German descent. Do I want to be referred to as an Italian-Irish-German-American or any variation of the three? Of course not!

While I am proud of my diverse heritage, I want to be simply identified as an American. I happen to be white. If I were black, does that make me any less of an American? Of course not, unless we allow that to happen through the attempts of others to divide us.

So when speaking of Americans, why do we not refer to everyone in that way, instead of choosing to separate us or divide us along race identity? Are we not simply all part of the human race? I am not trying to oversimplify this, but we have to move past this.

Recently, I came across a poetic commentary written by an American icon, John Wayne. I was very moved by this, especially when hearing the audio, which you can easily find through an Internet search.

Please read the following excerpt very carefully and truly evaluate its value in today's world, even though it was written in the early 1970s. I encourage you to find and read the entire writing.

> The hyphen, *Webster's Dictionary* defines, is a symbol used to divide a compound word or a single word.
>
> So it seems to me that when a man calls himself an "Afro-American," a "Mexican-American," "Italian-American," an "Irish-American," "Jewish-American," what he's saying is, "I'm a divided American."
>
> United we stand ... divided we fall. We're Americans ... and that says it all. (—John Wayne, circa 1972)

I find myself writing this chapter over the Fourth of July holiday weekend, which provokes even more thought on this crisis, in light of how our nation was born and has developed over the last 220-plus years.

As many have stated, we are not a perfect union, but we are far and away the very best this world has ever known. Think of a world without America!

Throughout history and with all of its success in conflicts with other nations, America has lost many brave lives yet has never sought to conquer the land of others but rather to secure and promote their liberty and sovereignty.

As previously stated, I am very concerned that many younger Americans, perhaps the millennials, may take the greatness of this nation for granted, meaning that they might think our way life is so rooted that it is there forever.

All of us should realize that America's greatness has never been at greater risk for so many reasons.

I am also concerned that this same segment of our population might think it is okay to enlist political correctness as a viable solution to a perceived injustice or a better way of expression and not cherish those American institutions and values of greatness that have created the freedoms that they enjoy today.

America has changed over our very short history, but it should change with *American correctness* as the guiding light, not with such narrow viewpoints as *political correctness*, which reduces our greatness as a republic based on personal freedoms.

Let's look at another example of political correctness where its advocates are trying to have a football team change its name because they believe it is offensive to Native Americans or American Indians. There's that division again!

Interesting enough, polls indicate that a majority of these proud Native Americans don't agree with this assertion. So why do these PC activists pursue this?

Well again, it is contrary to their narrow viewpoint, so it must be wrong, must be an injustice and therefore done away with!

As discussed, many politicians pursue this. Our current president, who also pursues this behavior, has allowed our US Patent and Trademark Office to remove the team's trademark protections for the use of this team's name. This has been taken to our court system where activist judges have upheld the USPTO's decision and again on appeal.

Yes, political correctness has also found its way into our nation's court system, with many judges ruling as activists, following their personal beliefs, ambitions, and agendas rather than being impartial and deciding cases solely based on our nation's laws.

As we conclude this chapter, I would like to stress that we are allowing a serious threat to our nation's safety when we allow political correctness to distract America from the real threat that radical Islamic terrorism is to our homeland.

Why does our president walk on eggshells when speaking around the real issue that some of the Muslim faith, who are radical Islamists, seek only to kill innocent Americans, either here or abroad?

Why does he insist on not identifying this enemy for who they are, rather than describing them as "lone gunmen" or their attacks as "workplace violence"?

Even when the evidence is clear that those involved in these deadly acts against America are radical Islamic terrorists, President Obama still remains silent and maintains his hardened ideology.

This is extremely puzzling given these enemies describe themselves as Islamic jihadists. This is not a reason to assume all of the Muslim faith support this twisted perversion of Islam, but let's be clear eyed here and understand that these radicals will kill not only those of non-Muslim faith but other Muslims as well!

Shutting down honest discussion of this problem and leaving Americans vulnerable, simply because of PC nonsense, has allowed dangerous radicalization within our borders to take root, which is exploited by our enemies.

Recently, we suffered a tragedy where five of our military, four marines and one sailor, were targeted and murdered while working at two recruitment centers in Chattanooga, Tennessee.

The killer was a foreign-born American man, twenty-four years old, who had been radicalized by "extremist and radical Islamic beliefs."

I bring this up because, again, our president refused to acknowledge this attack on our military and citizenry for what it really was and, adhering to political correctness, simply described it as random violence.

I believe his reluctance is rooted in his determination to convince America that he and his policies have eliminated the threat of radical Islam and those who perpetrate it.

That could not be further from the reality of this threat.

It took our president five days to order our nation's flag to half-staff after this attack, and he did so only after public outcry and criticism.

The other concerning revelation of this tragedy was that our military members are not allowed to carry weapons while assigned to these recruitment centers.

These attacks on our military installations here in America are not a new occurrence, so why have our president and those he appoints to assess these threats to our nation not taken the proactive and appropriate steps to ready these military targets to properly defend themselves?

Those leaders that follow political correctness are failing our nation time and time again!

Is it not obvious, that political correctness in this example aids our enemies in their pursuits by suppressing thought and freezing our ability to take appropriate action?

So you can see how our own poor decisions, if allowed to continue, threaten our freedoms that many in the world seek to eliminate.

So again the question, why is political correctness a crisis for America today? Very simply, as you see from our discussions in this chapter, it creates division and not unity in America, which our enemies will and have exploited.

Political correctness seeks to diminish the greatness of America.

If we don't resist those tendencies of silent thought, we may never realize what is at stake for America.

I am not suggesting, as I have stated in earlier chapters, that you allow this to consume every aspect of your daily life, but it will take your attention and analysis to truly understand its potential for disastrous consequences for our nation.

Remember—American correctness will win the day and will provide the guidance we need as a nation!

# Chapter 5

## AMERICAN CRISIS NUMBER THREE
## RACE RELATIONS IN AMERICA

This is the crisis that concerns me the most at this time in our history as a nation.

In the twentieth century, we were fortunate to have Dr. Martin Luther King Jr. come along at the right place and time for our country. MLK was an American leader, as much as he was a leader for the civil rights movement of the 1960s.

Not only was he a leader of quality, but he was truly an inspirational leader with the fortitude and conviction of his beliefs. I still get goose bumps every time I hear his "I Have a Dream" speech.

MLK created an awakening for this country, but even with all of the roadblocks and humiliation he encountered, he still chose to lead peaceful protests in the spirit of unity, not division. He was truly an American hero.

We need a Martin Luther King for the twenty-first century, and we need it now!

Sadly, President Obama could have been this leader, but as I said earlier, he has chosen a different path than MLK as it relates to race relations in America.

I know some will disagree and say that he was elected as our president and not to champion a civil rights issue or race relations and that he has to govern all of America, certainly not choosing sides. Well, let's think about that.

I would say to those who challenge my assertion, if this were true, that he as our president should not get involved in race, then why has he chosen to pick and choose when he does inject himself—and only then in highly racially charged incidents across America?

Unfortunately, our president has chosen a path that divides Americans along race. He has injected himself not to unify but rather to divide.

MLK sought to look to the future where race would no longer be a wedge between Americans, and he urged America to consider the content of our character and not the color of our skin. Sound familiar?

Martin Luther King and all of those who stood with him, through unwavering conviction, overcame the institutional racial discrimination that existed in America. They set the stage for future generations to build on that success and move this country forward in unity.

Many in today's America who are in a position to unite and build on prior achievements have failed these courageous leaders of the 1960s.

Unfortunately, some who stood with MLK still choose only to focus on the past injustices when speaking to today's America instead of speaking to the future that MLK envisioned.

This country has memorialized MLK with a national monument in the form of his statue and a national holiday to celebrate his birthday. This will forever be a tribute to him, standing alongside America's other great monuments and leaders.

Is this not a tremendous achievement for a country that was so troubled by the institutional racism of the twentieth century?

So why do we not take advantage of these tangible achievements to shape the correct path forward as a united America?

I believe that if MLK were here to see the lack of progress after all that he sacrificed, he would say, "Don't just celebrate me on one day in January every year, but rather embrace my spirit of unity every day and move forward to vanquish racism of all kinds in America!"

Our current president is among those in a position to have a profound and positive influence on this crisis, but he has failed and chooses to look backward and not find ways to move forward to unite in an inspiring way as MLK did.

He insists on highlighting only the racial wrongs of the past, while always trying to tie these wrongs to present-day interactions between black and white Americans.

He is especially outspoken and critical of our nation's law enforcement when we see an officer interact with someone in the black community. Facts or no facts, he insists on citing racism as the only reason for police interaction with blacks.

Have you noticed that our president speaks briefly and infrequently about the enormous strides forward that this country has accomplished?

Ask yourself, what are his real motives?

He surrounds himself with others who have failed to unite, such as Al Sharpton, who self-identifies as a civil rights leader. When have you ever heard this individual try to unite America—all America and not just black America?

And let there be no mistake, Al Sharpton does not try to unite black America but rather incites black America toward anger and hatred. This individual is not a leader for America, and for our president to validate him as a leader is counterproductive and disingenuous.

So why is all this happening? Well, sadly, as I stated earlier, our president chooses to politicize every crisis we encounter, meaning he uses these crises to promote his political party's agenda and ideology over the well-being of this nation.

Let me stress that I am not being naïve as it relates to the practice of politics by politicians! However, all Americans must think clearly when evaluating the use of this tactic in terms of race relations, which can harm and stifle American greatness.

A president should be the last to employ this tactic if he or she is truly an American leader.

Let's go back for a minute to my assertion that President Obama could have been instrumental in the creation of an MLK moment for the twenty-first century.

Our black communities in the inner cities of America are in great turmoil. If our president had spent just a small amount of his time—in a consistent, well-intentioned way—finding ways to inspire those who feel left out of society, we would be further ahead rather than further behind with respect to racial tensions in our country.

Think of it. America had just elected its first black president. Who better than he to excite those in the black community who felt disenfranchised from America?

Who better than he to inspire people to challenge themselves to rise above the thoughts of racial inequality?

Who better than he to speak honestly about the greatness of a country that, after all the racial struggles of the twentieth century, elected a black man as president in the twenty-first century?

Who better than he to speak to those who chose the path of crime and self-destruction to instead choose the path of hard work and personal responsibility?

I am deeply disappointed that there have been so many lost opportunities for all of America to rise above these challenges, simply because a few so-called leaders choose politics and/or division over meaningful conversation and change.

So why has America allowed this to happen? Many Americans have just accepted those powerful sound bites of hate and mistrust rather than truly think through this problem.

America has to stop speaking in terms of minority and majority with respect to the races of its citizens. This is only exploited by those who seek to divide and attempt to diminish America's progress in overcoming racial tensions.

Those that target America's consciousness to promote racial strife and division solely to advance their own agendas and personal ambitions are despicable and should be removed from the discussion.

Look at some recent cases where there has been a white police officer and a black American, which tragically ended in the death of the black American.

In these examples, consider how all the misinformation and distrust has further divided America.

Consider how all of the deception perpetrated by some has only created more rioting, more destruction of property, more hate, more distrust, and a further breakdown of societal norms.

I want to stress that many of those in our news media have done nothing to expose these bad actors at both the national and local levels of government. In many cases, they choose to follow the same twisted narrative of those who choose division.

Remember how insidious it is to ignore the critical facts and simply promote falsehoods as credible news accounts of these life-changing events in our society.

Additionally, look at how these same purveyors of division sought only to discredit our nation's law enforcement without any effort to honor these same men and women who provide our public safety.

This deception only further raised tensions and added to the violence!

I am always motivated to stay positive that America can solve this crisis when I hear black Americans speak to this crisis in an honest and profound way. They attempt to speak to the minds and hearts of all Americans, not just black America.

These leaders might be just an everyday American trying to live his or her life to the fullest. They could be local or national politicians, or they could be people in education, law enforcement, or the clergy. Whoever they are, they should be heard by all of America and without others trying to silence their voices.

I mentioned before that if you criticized President Obama and you were white, many, especially in our media, would label you as a racist.

Have you noticed then when a black person states a position or promotes a narrative that is different from those who seek to divide us along race, he or she is called some of the most vicious names imaginable. They are referred to as "Uncle Tom," "not authentically black," "sellout," and on and on.

These black Americans would rather lead as Martin Luther King Jr. did and look for ways to bring us forward rather than backward, which if we allow it, could destroy the nation we all love and cherish.

These same black Americans have not forgotten America's past or racial struggles, but they would rather to look to the future for ways to bring America together and not simply wipe out our past experiences.

Unfortunately, pursing racial strife and perceived racial injustice has become a way of life in this country for some who choose to profit from it or gain national prominence. Some in politics use this division solely to create voting blocs to ensure their reelection.

What I just described in the last paragraph is a great example of how some seek to manipulate thought in order to further their personal ambitions when they have no real interest in solving a crisis or helping the people affected. They are only interested in our mindless agreement with their views—and only their views!

Think about these motivations and ask yourself, are these purveyors of racial strife in any way concerned about solving this crisis? Sadly, no!

Those in politics and those so-called civil rights leaders shape their messages to promote despair and distrust among the very people that are hurt the most. Yet sadly, these same people believe these so-called leaders are acting in their best interest.

A person who chooses to stay uniformed and not seek the truth, who instead blindly accept falsehoods, is the most vulnerable. Unfortunately, there is a large segment of these individuals of every race in our country.

As silent thought becomes the norm, the greater the risk that our thought will harden in place, and what we see, hear, and read will not penetrate our consciousness. You can see examples of this throughout your day if you pay close attention to exchanges between people.

Do not kid yourself; some politicians and those who support them will take advantage of this and exploit it to the fullest extent possible.

After the tragedy in Ferguson, Missouri, the phrase "black lives matter" became a recurring statement by blacks, whites, activists, and politicians, with many in the media repeating it as well.

How many of these same politicians, civil rights leaders, activists, and those in the media have you heard express the same concerns for all of the senseless killing as a result of black-on-black crime in our inner cities across this nation? Their silence is staggering!

Why was the tragedy in Ferguson, where a white police officer shot a young black man, more important to these same so-called leaders and some in the media?

Why do they speak so loudly about this and stay silent about the loss of black lives when taken by other blacks?

Do those black lives not matter?

This loss of life does not matter to those with personal or political agendas and those who do not have any concern for a unified American agenda!

A serious barrier to honest conversation about this crisis is that if you do not agree, you might be labeled as a racist or a sellout, which shuts downs debate very quickly.

Many Americans simply choose to sit back and hope for change but do very little else to engage in this discussion.

I believe the way to start to solve this crisis is for us to look only to leaders, both black and white, who believe in unity, not division. As stated earlier, thought for many of us has really hardened!

Those who promote silent thought (meaning they don't want you to challenge their viewpoints, wanting you to simply accept them) have so inflamed racial tensions that not only do people's thoughts harden, but their hearts harden as well!

The keys to unlock this are difficult to find, but equally difficult is to reestablish the trust between different races. This American problem has gone unaddressed for quite some time.

However, when speaking openly about it, you can look to many personal success stories that have lifted many from despair to fully enjoying the American dream in a colorblind society.

The opportunities for meaningful change when President Obama took office were plentiful but were not acted on. Additionally, throughout his tenure in office, he was provided with additional opportunities to act in of all America's interest.

Time and time again, our president has used these as opportunities to further divide America in a very deceptive way, only citing income inequality and racial inequality to build a voting bloc that sees race through one lens.

He and those who support his motives don't believe in finding ways to expand life's opportunities for these segments of our population. They prefer to promote despair and envy, which can only lead to distrust and hate.

These politicians that promote racial strife believe that they can manipulate many in our black community, especially in our inner cities, by providing government programs that hold people in place, rather than providing pathways to self-reliance and personal growth.

These same politicians, when speaking about adding more people to welfare programs, act as if it is a badge of honor. This is not something to celebrate; rather, these leaders should be embarrassed for failing to lead all of America and find ways to lift those out of poverty and despair.

I am not understating the importance of our country being a compassionate nation and having appropriate government programs, safety nets for the poor and those caught in an endless cycle of despair.

But you see, some of our politicians and civil rights leaders want to create and continue dependency, which they believe will maintain a reliable voting bloc, which will keep these politicians in office and these civil rights leaders relevant.

I cannot stress this enough. These political tactics are some of the most destructive to our nation's unity, more so than any other crisis facing our country.

Is it any wonder that we continue to see rioting and unrest in these communities? As I stated earlier, when one's thought and heart hardens, despair and distrust will settle in, and violence will erupt.

Look at the rioting and destruction in Baltimore, Maryland, after six police officers, three white and three black, were accused of causing the death of a black man while in police custody.

In Baltimore, at the time of this unrest, you had a black mayor, a black police commissioner, and a black state's attorney. Yet these protestors still felt the need to riot and destroy property. Why?

This provides one of the most vivid examples of how those who seek to manipulate our thoughts and advance their own political and personal ambitions and agendas can so easily influence others to reject objective thought, the rule of law, and basic common sense.

This was another example of where some used this tragedy to promote distrust of law enforcement, which only accomplished more violence and destruction.

The mayor of this city, in a press conference during the unrest, actually stated, "We provided space for those who wished to destroy, the space to do that," then tried to insist that she did not make this statement.

She also instructed her police department to not engage the rioters and hold in place, functionally telling law enforcement officers to stand down. Many officers were injured as a result, and there was extensive damage to private and public property.

Baltimore's police commissioner denied these nonengagement orders given to his police force during these protests.

This mayor also made the comment that this incident was a difficult balancing act.

Really!

What allowed this situation to spiral out of control? Was it due the incompetence of this mayor?

Is the answer not very obvious?

Thankfully, Maryland's governor stepped in and called up the National Guard to assist in bringing order to this volatile situation.

Baltimore's mayor did not provide leadership, and while observing her handling of this incident, it was apparent how arrogant she was and how unfit she was to deal with this unrest. I do wonder if she had any communication with President Obama's administration during this protest and rioting.

Baltimore's state's attorney also displayed her incompetence in the early stages of this incident, acting more as an activist against perceived racial injustice than as a state's attorney that should only be concerned with the pursuit of legal justice for all.

Through her remarks, it became obvious that she was more concerned with personal ambitions and her own agenda than truly pursuing the justice that is demanded of the office she holds.

What have these political leaders and those of their political party done while in office to foster trust in our legal system by those who instead chose violent protest and rioting?

When did any of these political leaders in Baltimore attempt to speak to those rioting, to appeal for respect of law and order?

In the weeks that followed, Baltimore experienced very high numbers of black-on-black killings. Why would this happen?

Have these people who choose crime been emboldened by the ineptitude of Baltimore's leaders during the recent protests and riots?

Is the morale in Baltimore's police department so low as a result of this mayor's behavior and her lack of support for these brave men and women that they choose not to police actively and look the other way?

Think about it. Other police departments across the nation, such as the NYPD, have also lost confidence in their mayors for the same reasons.

There is no question that our nation's law enforcement agencies can experience neglect or discriminatory behavior by some in their ranks, but this is the rare exception and not the norm when dealing with all Americans, white and black alike.

These incidents are dealt with as they occur with disciplinary action and retraining, but we should be certain that our law enforcement members are policing themselves as well as our communities.

Our leaders, both local and national, must support law enforcement and speak strongly to all citizens that our law enforcement professionals are there for the common good and must be respected at all times.

Here again was another opportunity for our president to present a positive message to those in Baltimore that feel the need to pursue a life of crime and violence instead of being law-abiding citizens.

This is occurring within minutes of our White House, a forty-five-minute drive, or even quicker in Marine One.

But again, he has failed to act as a leader to inspire and instead remains silent!

Even if President Obama did not want to concede on his insistence to only highlight racial tensions, why not take this opportunity to speak to those who have abandoned family values, personal growth, and responsibility and encourage them to instead embrace these ideals?

Why would he not use his advantage of being the first black president and his "bully pulpit" to reach as many black Americans as possible with a positive message of hope and inspiration rather than the continuing theme of despair?

Why would he not want to inspire as many black Americans as possible to take the path that he followed of hard work, perseverance, and sacrifice, and then highlight the results of these choices with his personal successes, strong family values, and, of course, his being elected the forty-fourth president of the United States of America?

Please do not let anyone attempt to convince you otherwise or allow him or her to target your thoughts with distractions and excuses.

Every American should question his motives and realize how destructive his message of division has been and how his silence has harmed so many who need positive reinforcement and the courage to change the paths they are on and reject crime and violence.

I firmly believe that the root of the violence in our communities starts with the breakdown of the family unit. Every American begins his or her life in innocence and without any of these antisocial tendencies.

However, if our children are not raised with the care and love required to instill life's critical values and morality, along with the unity and equality that MLK embraced, they will not take the correct path toward adulthood. They will fail and fall into a cycle of dependency and crime.

Even if a parent is doing his or her best to raise his or her children, oftentimes it is counteracted by outside influences. For example, a struggling single parent is trying to speak to his or her adolescent or young adult child about life experiences, personal responsibilities, and how to behave in and outside the home.

Yet all this child or young adult is exposed to outside of the home is an onslaught of distorted views that promote distrust and despair, speak only about racial inequality, income inequality, and distrust for law enforcement and anything white!

In addition to these distorted viewpoints, these children and young adults become addicted to not only drugs in some cases but also the perceived easier path of crime, dealing drugs, and a gangster or thug mentality.

America must deal with this issue; we cannot ignore it. It will not go away, and we must not fail!

Think back to the Michael Brown tragedy in Ferguson, Missouri. Who failed this young man in his formative years? What allowed this young man to think it was okay to steal and, most importantly, that it was okay to fight with a police officer for the officer's gun and assault the police officer along with his friend?

During the entire incident and the violent unrest that followed, how many times did you hear anyone asking questions about why this young man's path did not take him in a different direction other than crime and having no respect for law enforcement?

The silence was alarming.

Please do not be distracted by those who deny or talk around this assertion by saying that Michael Brown was victimized by racial discrimination.

Unfortunately, this is just one tragedy along with so many other senseless deaths occurring in our black communities.

Does the fact that these inner-city communities are no longer spoken about in the press or by those purveyors of racial strife and division mean that the violence, crime, and despair have ceased?

Of course not. So again, where are these same individuals that shouted so loudly that black lives matter?

They are not interested in these deaths because they do not further their disingenuous agendas and personal ambitions. Sadly, lives are still being lost at alarming rates, yet now these lives are no longer visible.

Please consider the high number of abortions among blacks in our inner cities. Do these black lives not matter as well?

Look at the unacceptably high rates of unemployment among blacks in our inner cities.

Look at the unacceptably high rates of poverty and crime among these same Americans.

Let's be clear. The racial tensions and crime that exist in our inner cities, especially in the black communities across our nation, require a unified approach by many in America in order to overcome.

We drastically need a catalyst to ignite a true determination to move forward in the ways MLK dreamed of and fought for!

This catalyst must be so powerful it can soften the hardened thoughts and hearts of those that follow the path of self-destruction, so that positive reinforcement for change has a chance to enter their consciousness.

We have to ask ourselves, what political party is in control of these cities where the crime and racial unrest is the highest across our nation? Are we allowing political agendas to make this problem worse?

We have to stop this endless cycle of dependency by many in these inner-city communities and motivate those trapped there to reach for greater fulfillment in life rather than accepting the status quo. Government dependency, without understanding or believing in the values of personal responsibility, hard work, and self-worth, will only create more dependency, despair, and envy, followed by crime in many cases.

Ask yourself, why would our president undermine the work requirements for those on public assistance through executive decisions?

Do he and his supporters really believe that this policy to eliminate work requirements promotes greater personal responsibility?

Sadly, no! They are intentionally creating more dependency, believing that in doing so, it will further ensure that those affected will vote for them and their failed policies.

Please evaluate this honestly. How could dependence on government handouts ever be more rewarding than the experience of personal independence and all the successes that can follow?

Those trapped in this generational cycle of despair, who are not committing any crime and are struggling to find the pathway to a better standard of living, are in a constant state of fear of the extreme violence and drugs that have overtaken their neighborhoods.

Those disingenuous community leaders and politicians and those in the news media that only denigrate and call into question the motives and character of those in law enforcement are making a very bad situation that much worse.

If we lose control over law and order, we are sure to fail as a nation!

Let's be clear. There are some that seek only to commit violent crime and reject established social norms, and these individuals should be dealt with firmly and fairly within our justice system.

However, we cannot fail to look at the root cause for this breakdown of personal conduct and the bad choices that follow and take actions to reverse this downward spiral toward self-destruction.

We have to address these root causes and deal with those that break our laws at the same time. One without the other will not give us the space and time to overcome these problems for black and white alike.

When we look at the nonviolent segments of our society with respect to race, we see differences between our older and younger generations.

Of our older generation, let's say the older baby boomers and older, many have experienced or witnessed racial discrimination in their lifetimes.

I would like to believe that many older Americans recognize that this period was very difficult for blacks in America but have also seen the many successes in eliminating racism, starting from the days of MLK to our present time.

They also believe in America's determination to eradicate racism of any type in our nation and allow America to heal and move forward in unity.

Sadly though, there are those who still harbor hate and mistrust, both among whites and blacks. Their thoughts and hearts remained hardened, in a place and time that no longer exist.

They will not allow themselves to find the honest and productive path forward—not to forget these past injustices but to look the future in unity.

In all fairness, it is very difficult for anyone to look forward when you have so many so-called political and civil rights leaders, as well as many in our news media, acting as if racism is still dominating our society.

And they are doing so for all the wrong reasons, as discussed earlier in this chapter.

Sure, America will always experience some random act of discrimination, as we are a very diverse nation, and there will always be someone who hates another simply because of a different ethnicity or color or faith.

I believe through attrition we will resolve the stubbornness of some of our older generation, as some may never change their minds, no matter what message they are listening to.

Our younger generations do not view race the same way our older generations do but are still very susceptible to targeted thought by those who profit from division and identity politics.

If our country were left to evolve naturally, without this insidious intervention by narrow-minded politicians and so-called civil rights leaders who only foster hate and division, our younger generations would overcome this problem.

It may take another generation or two to fully solve it, but I believe it is doable.

Is it not encouraging whenever you see our very young children, black and white, playing together without ever thinking of race or color?

Of course they wouldn't, unless they are encouraged to do so by others who wish to target their thought with hate and dishonesty rather than love and inspiration.

Sure, our young children probably notice a difference in color but not through the lens of any racial bias.

You also see this in our younger generation at an older age as well. They simply don't consider race as a barrier to relationships and pursuing mutual interests as friends or colleagues.

Our thought creates lenses through which we see others. Unfortunately, in many cases our lenses do not flip forward, allowing the colorblind lens to flip into place.

Make no mistake in thinking that, through this crisis, the purveyors of racial strife and division will continue to target all Americans, especially our younger generation, with these divisive tactics to promote distrust and hate.

I want to stress that I know that some may disagree with my assertions on this crisis and argue that my thoughts are too simplistic. Please challenge their viewpoint and remember that when honesty guides us, the solutions are simple and straightforward!

We just need the courage to act and believe in America's greatness to overcome this challenge.

So in closing this chapter, I encourage those who want to be part of an MLK moment for our country, please step forward!

President Obama, America is waiting!

# Chapter 6

# AMERICAN CRISIS NUMBER FOUR
# POLITICS IN AMERICA

As we prepare to discuss this crisis, I ask you to reflect on the previous chapters on the crises facing America, looking at how interconnected they really are.

In this chapter, we will see how our politics and those who hold political office can have a dramatic effect on the causes of and solutions for the crises that I have identified in this book.

If I were to say, "We the people need to take back Washington (by Washington, I mean our government in Washington, DC). We the people need to change our political system," do these sound like radical or extremist comments?

They may, and I can understand if you think they are. They are not radical or extreme in the sense that they would result in an act of violence or not following the rule of law.

However, these are radical and extreme statements that express the seriousness of this crisis. Our American political system is in crisis and requires the attention of every American.

It is extremely important for every American to understand that we are not just a democracy; we are also a constitutional republic, where power is vested in its citizens and not the politicians we elect.

It is also important to remember that just because a majority of politicians pass a law, we should not assume it is lawful under our constitution, simply due to a majority decision in Congress followed by the signature of our president.

When considering a US Supreme Court decision, here again, just because a majority of nine justices decide to uphold or strike down a matter before them, we should not assume their decision is lawful under our constitution.

However, this is difficult to challenge, due to how our constitution was written, which makes their decision the law of the land.

We will speak about our US court system, including the US Supreme Court and how politicized it has become later in this chapter.

How often do you think about politics, either local or national? Daily? Only occasionally? Only leading up to an election? Briefly after hearing or reading a short sound bite? Or really never at all?

I would like to stress that simply allowing a questionable sound bite from a newscast or the front page of newspaper to enter your consciousness is not thinking about politics but rather is allowing the opinions of others to possibly form your opinion, which you may or may not repeat as if it were your opinion.

Remember the concepts of silent thought and targeted thought and how damaging they can be if you do not challenge your thought process and the validity of what you decide to allow to enter and take root in your consciousness.

Let me stress that I am not judging anyone's decision to accept these opinions or so-called news accounts if you happen to agree with them. Every American is free to think and believe anything he or she chooses to.

However, my goal, as stated several times earlier, is to promote critical thought analysis when considering the crises discussed in this book.

So back to whether we are really thinking about politics. Why would we, especially when for many of us it appears in the abstract and not worthy of our daily thought activities?

Yet we should understand that everything in life that we enjoy and everything we don't is in one way or another driven by local and national politicians and their actions.

As we continue in this chapter, we will focus more on national politics and those politicians. However, please do not fail to consider your local and state political institutions. Some are working in their community's best interest, but many are in crisis.

This is a result of them being closer to the people they represent, but make no mistake, unless we hold them accountable, they will move further from the people they represent and closer to serving only themselves.

When we consider politics and the actions of specific politicians in our daily lives, it is important that we understand that they are not always acting in our best interest or that of our nation.

Then whose interest are they concerned with?

Is it their own political careers, their respective party affiliation and its ideology, special interest groups who donate to their campaigns, or the leaders in their respective chambers such as the US Senate and House of Representatives?

Yes to all—and probably other reasons that we are not aware of but are certainly not in our best interest.

But ask yourself, who elected these individuals to their respective offices?

We the people—right? Well, not necessarily!

So why would they not consider only our interests and those of our nation when fulfilling the duties of their office?

Several reasons.

The biggest and most disturbing reason is that many of our politicians have forgotten and really choose to ignore that they are public servants elected to office to serve our interests rather than serving their own personal ambitions and careers.

They have forgotten or fail to recognize that public service was not meant to be a career path to enrich oneself while in office and, more specifically, after leaving office.

Time and time again, we have seen newly elected politicians enter their office with the highest of ethical standards and transparency with the American public, but they are either corrupted and then follow those who hold power, or they try to lead and remain true to their higher standards of conduct.

Unfortunately, those that try to lead and serve the interests of those who elected them are marginalized by the corrupt nature of our current political system.

It is very important to understand how the targeted thought of others plays a very large role in our voting decisions, especially by those who seek higher offices, such as state governors, those in Congress, and our president.

Not only do these politicians target our thought, but all of those who support them and their party do as well.

Also, as we have discussed earlier, depending on their party affiliation, many in our news media support one party over the other rather than just impartially reporting on every candidate and public policy.

As each of these campaigns move through their primary contests and get closer to Election Day, we are barraged with endless print and television ads, along with the opinions of political pundits and, in many cases, biased opinions disguised as news.

All of this is done in an effort to persuade you to cast your vote in their favor.

Ask yourself, isn't it interesting how visible we are to these politicians when they are in need of our vote but so invisible to them after they win election?

If we allow others to target our thought process and then cast our vote without validating whether or not it is in our best interest and that of our nation, who is really voting?

So you see, we have not really elected this politician. Sure we are the ones who entered the polling place and cast the vote.

But if we simply yielded to outside influences without spending time evaluating a candidate's true motives and qualifications, the ballot we cast is not ours but is that of someone else who directed our action in their interest!

We have now become their instrument to achieve their objectives, and in doing so, we have put at risk our identity and our freedoms under our constitution.

Let's be clear here. To win, politicians must target our thoughts, and that's okay. We want those asking for our vote to explain their reasons for seeking office and to present their qualifications for us to examine.

However, we must be very discerning when considering these national elections and resist the temptation to simply accept quick sound bites to form our decision regarding whom to vote for.

Our greatest right and our most important responsibility as Americans is to cast our vote as a well-informed citizen, with not only our interest in mind but serious concern for the interests of this great nation.

I strongly encourage you to not vote simply on a straight party line, meaning that we do not necessarily consider the candidate and instead only vote for everyone within a certain party affiliation, such as Democrat, Republican, Libertarian, or Independent.

To do so is just another example of how our vote can be manipulated. Consider how many in certain parties try to take advantage of this tendency by demeaning others simply because they identify with a particular party.

They use this tactic to unnecessarily divide America while at the same time believing they will create additional power and control for their party through practicing identity politics.

Additionally, they exploit this tendency and know that a certain percentage of voters will cast their vote for party affiliation rather than consider all candidates fairly.

The days where a political party has earned and deserves our faith and trust are nonexistent in today's political system. Unfortunately, many of today's politicians and those who support them play fast and loose with the truth.

Please pay special attention to politicians and those who support them when listening to their comments; they only demean their opponents instead of honestly debating the issue with them.

Those who employ this tactic are very good at deception and do not want an honest exchange of ideas!

Politicians, especially those in Washington, DC, have shown us many times over that they will put their own personal ambitions above those that have elected them—and by extension our country.

Politics by its nature creates division and opposition, which is why we must pay more attention to this crisis at this time, more than at any other time in our nation's history!

We must take the dramatic steps that will change our American political system. But we can only accomplish this with a unified approach and with the attention of all of America.

Many of our politicians have become so entrenched in their respective office and party that they are now failing America with far greater frequency. Remember my comment about how we become invisible after they secure our vote. Think about it!

Think about all the policy positions stated and promises made during a campaign, and then after elected, consider how many of these politicians actually did what they promised and now only engage in excuses and double-talk.

When considering the major challenges facing our country, we must no longer readily accept their actions and words as correct and trustworthy but rather dissect their actions and words in order to determine their true intent and value.

I know this all sounds very cynical on my part, but we have to come to the realization that our government in Washington, DC, has become totally dysfunctional and in many cases very corrupt.

The reasons for this are many. However, the genesis for this dysfunction is that everything is so politicized. Contradictory—right?

Not when you consider that what I mean by the overpoliticization of our government is that these so-called leaders in Washington take actions with their own party and political futures in mind.

This is why at this point every American must resist the tendency of silent thought, meaning that we have to find the time to challenge our thought processes in order to truly understand the nature of this crisis.

To only accept the opinions of a small group of politicians in Washington, those who support them, and those in our news media with political motives transfers control of our destiny to those few in Washington!

If we do not have an honest conversation with ourselves about how much we understand and what we do not understand about national politics, we will never find ourselves in a position of strength and confidence to deal with this crisis effectively.

Please do not ignore this crisis and expect someone else to solve the problem!

Believe me, these politicians exploit this apathy on our part and will only continue to deceive, until they realize that we have taken a proactive mind-set to hold them accountable as public servants.

Have you ever wondered why politics in Washington has to be so complicated?

Well, it doesn't have to be.

Let's go back to the national leaders I referenced in an earlier chapter. In addition to President Obama, we had John Boehner (until the fall of 2015), the speaker of the House of Representatives, and Nancy Pelosi, the minority leader in the House of Representatives.

Then in the US Senate, we have Mitch McConnell, the majority leader, and Harry Reid, the minority leader.

Then you have several others in both chambers that compose their respective leadership teams.

These so-called leaders in the House of Representatives and the US Senate, along with our president, are collectively at the root of the dysfunction in Washington.

Some are worse than others due to the divisive tactics they employ. But they are all responsible for this dysfunction. I encourage you to closely watch how they conduct themselves and participate in this failure to serve America.

When I use the word *leaders* for those in Congress, I do not mean our leaders but rather that they are the leaders of their respective political parties.

These current leaders have all been in Congress for many years, and their leadership positions have changed during their tenure due to which party is in control. The amount of time they have each spent in

Washington highlights what is wrong with our national political system.

In the fall of 2015, John Boehner resigned from his office and the speakership, as many have challenged and questioned his leadership. Paul Ryan was elected speaker, and we will see if there is any positive change or just the same ineffective status quo!

We elect these politicians to office and then assume they will in good conscience form their teams, either in the majority or the minority.

Unfortunately, they have demonstrated their tendency to only allow those in their party who agree with their views to be a part of their leadership teams. This itself creates more unnecessary division.

This, along with the fact that many of these politicians have been in political office for far too long, only further complicates the political process.

So you can see very quickly how within each party we have factions that further divide and only make it harder to find consensus, not only within their own party but when dealing with the opposing party and then trying to get an important bill signed by the president.

Political control in Washington is determined by which party holds the majority in each of the Senate and House chambers, and of course the presidency.

We are primarily a two-party system, Democrat and Republican, with members in both parties holding different viewpoints, such as libertarian, liberal, and conservative, with varying degrees of intensity in each.

Over time, depending on which party has been in control of either the House or Senate, the controlling party has changed the procedural process, which in many cases has created more division and further complicates the entire political process.

Additionally, there are many special-interest groups lobbying Congress on a full-time basis in order to persuade members to initiate legislation or to vote a particular way.

These lobbyists are paid by outside groups that want to influence Congress and gain access to the process by supporting the reelections of many politicians.

Other factors in our political process are the actions of our president, who can either be a proponent or an opponent of legislation pending in Congress.

I would again remind you that our current president has very much been part of the breakdown in our political system, simply because he chooses to overpoliticize every view and action he takes, solely to achieve his personal agenda and ambitions.

Our political process was not meant to be any easy process, as our founding fathers understood the importance of passing legislation in the best interest of every American, realizing it would take honest debate and compromise.

However, they realized early on that the human spirit could be corrupted if allowed to act without checks and balances and believed that serving in public office was not meant to be a career choice but rather a desire to serve our nation and its interests.

Sadly, what we have today in Washington are politicians who are more concerned with their reelections and maintaining their power base than "we the people."

These politicians have lost their way and no longer serve America, serving only their personal ambitions and believing they are entitled to a lifetime in politics with impunity.

Tragically, they have abused our constitutional system of government and have instituted a corrupt political system with many unnecessary layers of complexity, which they know causes many Americans to simply look the other way!

These so-called leaders have so complicated the political process that it is often almost impossible for an important piece of legislation to reach the point where a vote can take place, due to endless politicization and polarization, followed by gridlock.

Have you ever wondered why so many times these so-called leaders find themselves at the eleventh hour facing a critical vote and yet in gridlock?

Then they politicize it, such as with threats of government shutdowns or with America unable to honor its financial commitments. They employ this tactic to distract and alarm America in the effort to again complicate the process and further their personal agendas.

Is this leadership? Of course not. It is only politics as usual in Washington!

Please do not believe that they act this way due to principled responsibility to the American people. In many cases, they are only acting to serve special-interest groups who assist them in winning reelection, followed by retaining or retaking power in the House and Senate.

Sure, they must seek and win reelection every two and six years, but for many of these career-minded only politicians, this is nothing more than a formality.

They have created a political apparatus that ensures their reelection by doing just enough for the respective districts and states, creating the impression that they are doing a good job and are worthy of reelection.

We have to understand that we are somewhat to blame when we continue to vote for politicians only because they bring a certain federal benefit to our local community or state, not taking the time to truly evaluate their real motives.

This is another instance where targeted and silent thought need to be considered, and we need to look at their impact on whether or not we are exercising our right to vote with critical thought and care for the nation we love.

Please bear in mind that the only thing that politicians do well is ensure their reelection.

These politicians are elected from a local perspective but then as a governing body in Washington are tasked with the responsibility to lead our country in the best interest of all Americans. They disappoint us time and time again and continue to deceive.

We should understand that these long-serving politicians may have come to Washington with interest in serving the voters that elected them and our country but now only serve themselves.

We are at a time where it has become very obvious that these politicians are human and thus imperfect, and they will continue to seek power if not checked by the American people.

So we now have to change this system, to ensure that we not only correct this crisis in the present but also ensure that it can never happen again.

We are a nation of laws and are granted certain rights under our constitution, which we exercise when we elect our fellow citizens to office and expect them to follow their constitutional responsibility after taking the oath of office.

Many politicians are not remaining true to that oath of office and have lost the trust and confidence of America.

So is it any wonder that we have lost confidence in our political system?

I know for many readers, the first part of this chapter may seem very obvious, and you may agree or disagree with my assertions. If you disagree, I encourage you to take some additional time to reconsider your opinion and please be objective in your thought process.

My goal is to put this crisis in perspective for everyone that reads this book and for everyone to challenge the status quo, what we believe is "normal" in Washington, DC.

This chapter is not only about stating the problems with our political system; it will also provide an achievable solution to this crisis.

That solution can be stated in just two words: term limits.

Now, I know that many will react and remind me that this has been talked about and considered before, and you are correct.

You may also remind me that we do have term limits, in the sense that our president can only serve two four-year terms, and those in Congress have to face the voting public every two and six years.

Yes, this is true, but it is not working, and many have found ways to overcome these constitutional restrictions for their own political gain and self-interest.

We must realize that many in Congress have decided that they will do anything to ensure they hold office and have now transformed public service into a lifetime career in politics, simply by corrupting our election process.

Let's consider our presidency and the current president and whether or not our constitutional term restriction of two four-year terms has been effective.

Have you ever thought about when our president starts to consider their reelection prospects?

It may surprise you, but I believe they are considering their second term while they are running for their first term as president.

Ask yourself, why would they not, especially if they have developed a winning political campaign and organizational structure across America? Why would they dismantle this after winning election and then, if choosing to run for reelection, have to reestablish this all over again?

Why would they not take advantage of the election results that showed where they did not win majorities and then take the next four years ensuring victory in the president's reelection campaign?

They wouldn't, so never believe presidents when they're asked if they will seek reelection and they answer that they have not made up their mind.

This is simply disingenuous, and we should be more alert to this deception and realize that every statement and action that a first-term president makes is guided by a desire to win a second term.

Additionally, we should think carefully about what our president may want to accomplish but will delay until they win reelection and no longer has to face the voting public as a consequence.

So you can see, the political deception starts very early on, and they will do and say anything to win reelection.

Is it not obvious that a president in the first term is simply doing and saying what they believe will win reelection and not necessarily acting in the best interest of America?

It should be, but it is amazing how many Americans do not recognize this deception and blindly accept every word, without thinking through it and considering whether there is any truth in these statements!

Think about it. In a president's first term, how much campaigning does a president engage in compared to how much actual governing takes place?

So back to term limits for the presidency. In essence, it is very important to limit how long one person can serve as president, as we have witnessed how easily power can corrupt those in Washington. However, we have to consider what value there is in having a president serve a second term.

Really think about this! If we believe that a president's first term is very carefully crafted to ensure reelection, then is America really benefiting in those first four years?

Sure, a first-term president is very active and does try to advance political agendas as well as persuade members of Congress and the American people to agree and follow their viewpoints.

But are the president's actions in the first term in the best interest of every American or are they only to repay the president's supporters and strengthen those of the same party affiliation?

I will cite our current president as an example of why a two-term presidency no longer works in today's political process. Think back to his first campaign for president. Do you remember all the promises of change and unity?

What change did he bring to Washington politics?

How much unity has he accomplished in Washington and throughout America?

It is very apparent that this president has not changed Washington politics and has made our political system even more divisive and more inept than ever before.

With respect to the question of how much unity he has accomplished, he has failed America. As a nation, we have never been more divided, and that makes it difficult to come together as a nation to take back Washington, as I earlier described.

Our president and many other politicians in both parties prefer a divided America, as they know the power of a united America would never stand for their failures.

After our current president won reelection in 2012, did we see any willingness to change politics or bring America together?

Sadly, no!

In addition, we see a president that has decided to sidestep our constitution and issue executive decisions to facilitate his own agenda and personal ambitions.

This lack of respect for our nation and its constitution was even more apparent after his party lost control of the US Senate in 2014.

If our president were honest with the American public during his campaign for his second term about the actions he was planning to take after winning reelection, do you honestly think America would have reelected him?

If your answer is yes, then ask yourself, why did he not express these views during his campaign for reelection?

As a president approaches the end of his second term, many refer to the president as a "lame duck," meaning the president in some ways becomes irrelevant or ineffective as he approaches the end of his presidency.

So let's reflect again on the value of allowing a two-term presidency.

Carefully consider a president's first term and how potentially deceptive it can be, not to mention all the endless fundraising and campaigning, and then in the second term all the potential for lawlessness that can go unchecked because the president does not have to face the voters again.

Is this really in the best interest of our nation?

Not only is it not in our best interest, but it does very little to address the crises we face as a nation.

Sure, our constitution provides for impeachment of our president, but in today's political environment, can we really implement this action?

Not easily, so we find ourselves having to live with the consequences of a failed presidency for eight years and then enduring more valuable time trying to reverse or correct the failed policies of a failed president!

My preference would be a single five-year term for the presidency.

I believe that this would limit the potential for abuse of office, distinguish those who truly wish to serve

America, and eliminate the need for the deception that a second term naturally produces.

Think about it. We have to accept that eight years is too long and that we are not getting any significant value from a president in the first term when they are only concerned with reelection, as I have described earlier.

Then in their second term, we see behavior that was disguised in their first term and a sense that they can violate our constitution with impunity. This, along with their concern for their legacy and not America, only furthers highlights how a second term is not in our best interest.

Our current president and his presidency is a vivid example of how two terms can fail to truly serve America.

I want to stress, that winning a second term is usually assured and has almost become a formality in today's political system.

We have to reshape our political system so that this important office attracts only those who possess a love of country and understand that holding this office is not a means to enhance personal statue but rather to preserve the greatness of America and that of its citizens.

Our president must possess humility and selflessness, not hubris and narcissism, must uphold our constitution at all times, and must never place personal ambitions above those of the American people.

I do believe that as we approach the 2016 presidential election, there are those seeking this office who do believe in these principles, so we should not lose faith in our nation's ability to solve this problem.

Let's now discuss those in Congress and term limits.

I want to stress that the requirement for those in Congress to face voters every two and six years does not solve the problem with our political system. Many politicians, especially those in their respective party's leadership, have found ways to win reelection easily.

I believe that having term limits is the only way to address the dysfunction in Washington and that it will fundamentally reshape our political system.

My preference for members in the House of Representatives would be a term limit restricted to five two-year terms, a total of ten years.

My preference for members in the US Senate would be a term limit restricted to two five-year terms, a total of ten years.

So as you can see, I believe in ten years in either the House or Senate, and then they are out. They will then have to go back to their communities and live under the laws they passed or did not pass while serving in Congress.

They could serve in both the House and the Senate but no more than ten years in total. For example, a House representative could serve two two-year terms in the House and then only one five-year term in the Senate.

After serving a total of ten years in either the House or Senate or a combination, they could seek the presidency and, if elected, serve the single five-year term.

In this case, it would be a total of fifteen years in Washington, and certainly a great deal of positive accomplishments could occur over fifteen years if the person is truly there to serve America and not just to enrich him or herself.

But think about this. With term limits in place, is it not more likely that someone would choose public service for the right reason and truly desire only to serve his or her constituents and America? Sure it is!

We have to remove any incentives for serving in public office that can result in personal wealth or power; otherwise we will continue to attract only those of questionable character.

It is very important to understand that just because politicians serve in an office for many years does not mean they are more knowledgeable and therefore would do a better job serving their constituents and the American people as a whole.

For many, the knowledge they gain is how to participate in this corrupt system of politics and nothing else—certainly not how to better serve America.

Too many years in Congress only accomplishes the opposite effect. They simply become career politicians with only their careers in mind and not the American people. Many of these politicians have become consumed by the prestige of holding national office.

Those that oppose term limits will argue with great intensity that long tenure in Washington is the only way Washington can work. Not only is this argument ridiculous, but look at the lack of results and the gridlock in Washington today!

Consider the records of the current leaders in the House and Senate that I cited earlier. These four politicians have collectively been in Washington for decades, in both majority and minority positions.

Ask yourselves, what have they done of a positive nature?

Sadly, very little!

But the damage they have done to our political system and our country has been enormous. As a result, America has completely lost trust and confidence in a system of government that was intended by our founding fathers to serve and protect the American way of life.

They have corrupted the greatest constitutional republic ever known to mankind, and not for any noble reason but simply to enrich themselves and those who support their deception.

Think about it. We are a nation of well over three hundred million people. Are we to believe that we have to accept these same failed politicians year after year and that there are not many who would do a far better job, if not for the closed nature and barriers to entry of this corrupt political system?

Please never be fooled by those who would oppose term limits, especially by those who hold office. They will say and do anything to hold on to their seats in Congress and their perceived power. They will target your thought process with deception and try to alarm you that term limits will create unnecessary turnover and chaos in Washington.

Again, utter nonsense!

Turnover in Washington is healthy for our nation, as it will bring new ideas and true patriotism to our Congress and presidency.

Think about a Washington where our politicians are only concerned with public service, transparency, and compromise. In restricting their terms in office, we are far more likely to see people serve for the right reason, rather than serve their personal interests.

I also believe that term limits will reduce the amount of money that has so much influence in Washington. We must remove as much outside influence as possible from our political system. The only influence on our politicians should be the will of the American people.

Special-interest groups provide a great deal of campaign coordination and contributions in a number of ways. This is one of the ways these entrenched politicians are assured of retaining their seats in Congress for decades without any real competition.

Oftentimes when politicians decide not to seek reelection, it is due to their desire to take their long political careers along with their rolodexes and transfer them to careers as lobbyists.

I can assure you that this behavior does not stem from a love of country, only for love of oneself!

I am not objecting to politicians deciding to leave politics and then seek careers to support themselves and their family.

What I am objecting to is a politician that has not served honestly while in Congress taking his or her political connections to a lobbying firm, simply to enrich him or herself at the expense of the American people.

Term limits may sound like a great idea, but I can assure you that it will not be easy to institute. We would have to amend our constitution, which would have to be initiated in Congress or by state legislatures through a national convention. Both paths are very difficult and take time.

I would prefer the path through Congress, as I believe it would identify the true political leaders and expose those who only seek to abuse their oath of office.

I feel very strongly that as we approach the 2016 presidential election cycle, if a candidate for president from either political party were to unconditionally accept and promote term limits, this solution would quickly find its way into America's consciousness.

Let me be very clear that I am not speaking about a candidate who would only briefly speak about term limits during a campaign stop. I am speaking about a candidate who would not only enthusiastically embrace term limits but unconditionally commit to the American public that he or she would only serve a single term if elected.

Additionally, I believe this candidate would win the presidency in a landslide election!

This candidate along with the American people must insist that the current party in control of both the House and Senate take up term limits and vote yes or no.

Every politician who either obstructs this vote or votes no should receive a no vote from America the next time he or she stands for reelection.

If both houses of Congress, by each reaching a two-thirds majority, propose an amendment to change term limits, our current president would probably oppose it, but not a problem.

The president does not have a say in this process and can only express his or her opinion. After Congress, the proposed amendment would then go to each of the state legislatures for ratification, requiring a three-fourths majority of states voting in favor to amend.

Again, all of those that refuse to vote or vote no would receive a no vote the next time they stood for reelection!

I assure you that this is not an easy process but is extremely necessary at this time, and our politicians in Washington will not do this on their own.

I can also assure you that if a majority of candidates running in 2016 for either the Senate or House for the first time embrace and commit to self-imposed term limits if elected, they will win their elections in great numbers.

I know many feel helpless, but we are not if we take a unified approach to solving this crisis. I am sure there may different ideas on how long these politicians should serve, but the only way to truly rid our political system of corruption and attract the right candidates is term limits.

I also know that many don't want to be bothered by this crisis and do not want to spend any significant amount of time thinking or speaking about it.

But think of it this way. Congress and our president should be expected to function normally and in our best interest, but they will not unless we create a framework that removes any ability for these politicians to become entrenched in Washington.

If we just spend the extra time and effort now as a unified America and solve this problem correctly, we can be assured that our political system will function properly without the need for our constant intervention.

As we move to close out this chapter, I want to spend some time on other negative consequences of a political system in crisis. We have seen how unnecessarily complicated and dysfunctional our Congress and presidency have become.

A serious concern is that through the dysfunction of those in Congress and that of our president, many if not all of our government agencies have become more layered with unnecessary complexity and bureaucracy and are failing to serve America.

Simply put, our federal government has become too large and is now incapable of self-correcting the inefficiencies that exist.

Think back to the two federal agencies I cited in an earlier chapter, the Veterans Administration and Internal Revenue Service.

Especially alarming is when we consider the VA hospitals and how poor management and the lack of oversight can diminish the quality of care our veterans receive—and in some cases whether a vet lives or dies.

How could this possibly happen and be allowed to continue?

It starts with the president and all the political appointments he makes, followed by his ability to manage these appointees.

Then there is Congress and its oversight responsibility.

They have both failed horribly with respect to the VA and with countless other examples, and why? Every action has become politically motivated, and every critical decision needed places a political calculation over that of good conscience and the well-being of America.

Another example of a federal agency that has become overpoliticized is our Department of Justice. This is extremely concerning, as this agency is tasked with ensuring that even our national politicians are not above the law, or are they?

Think about all the federal appointments made by our president and the extensive damage to America that can occur when a president only makes appointments out of political consideration and nothing else.

Consider the power over every American's life that our president has through his constitutional authority to make these appointments and only through a political lens.

Every federal judge is appointed by the president to serve lifetime terms. If our president only appoints these judges based on political calculations and their political beliefs, is this in America's interest?

Think about the potential for abuse and injustice by activist judges who only rule with a political motive in mind!

The greatest example of this is the president's power to appoint judges to the US Supreme Court. Look at how politicized this court of nine justices has become.

Almost every decision rendered by this court, irrespective of whether or not these nine justices have interpreted our constitution objectively, is determined by the political bias of these judges.

Congress does have a role in this process as these appointments by our president require the consent of the US Senate. The Senate will usually yield without too much opposition to cabinet appointments but will often times hold up appointments to the courts.

Do not ever believe that this process is not heavily driven by politics. It does not matter which party holds the majorities in Congress or which party holds the presidency, politics and political bias determine these outcomes.

This process of political appointment followed by congressional oversight is rooted in our constitution, and I am not suggesting that we try to amend this. It can work but not within this current political system.

However, I do want to highlight how an entrenched political class in Washington, left unchecked and allowed to serve too long, will only abuse this process and prevent it from ever serving America.

Two terms, eight years, for our president is too long and allows too much influence over this very important constitutional authority to name political appointees to these powerful positions in both the executive and judicial branches of our government.

With a Congress so dysfunctional and so consumed with only holding political power, the ability to oversee these appointments properly and safeguard America from potential abuses that can be taken by those appointed by the president is very much in question.

If, through their oversight responsibility, Congress finds abuse of office with any of these presidential appointments, they must be prepared to remove these individuals through the impeachment process.

But you see, if Congress is incapable of taking this action simply because of political and personal motives and not in honestly performing the duties of their office, then we will be destined to same failures in government as we have seen with this current administration and others before it, and for many years to come.

As stated earlier, with term limits for Congress, we will change the reason for one's desire to serve America, and I believe that anyone holding power in the executive or judicial branches of government who violates his or her oath of office would be removed quickly by this new breed of politicians.

Before we close this chapter, I want to finish a thought in an earlier chapter on the current front-runner for president in the Democrat party, Hillary Clinton.

During her time in politics as First Lady, US senator, and as secretary of state, she has demonstrated a total lack of respect for the American people through multiple transgressions, dishonesty, and deception.

I would be remiss if I did not cite this one individual as the most vivid example of how bad and how corrupt our political system has become.

This politician, along with her supporters and her acolytes, will do anything—and I mean anything—to win the presidency. They will target our thoughts with relentless intensity and deception.

Please think very carefully before and when considering this person for president!

In closing this chapter, I would like to remind my readers that patriotism and love of a country in Washington are not values that have been lost forever, but they have been temporarily suppressed by our current political system and can be restored.

When politicians fail, America will fail, unless we act!

# Chapter 7

# AMERICAN CRISIS NUMBER FIVE
# OPEN BORDERS AND IMMIGRATION

What is national sovereignty?

National sovereignty dates back to our founding as a nation in the American ideal of independence. Sovereign nations have the right to form governments, enact laws, and defend themselves against those nations that pose a threat to their sovereignty.

When we speak about sovereign borders, we speak about the lines that separate one country from another.

I believe it is very important when discussing this crisis that we keep these definitions in mind and how important these concepts are to the freedoms and liberty we enjoy each and every day.

As with the other crises discussed in this book, this crisis is no different in that it has become just as politicized as every other crisis discussed, possibly even more so.

When we speak about open borders and immigration, I do realize I am stating two separate points, but one is greatly affected by the other.

Let's start with open borders.

As a nation, we have open borders, meaning that we allow immigration for those wishing to come here— but within a legal process.

The open borders I am speaking about in this chapter refer to the unsecured southern border with Mexico, where millions have entered our country illegally.

Fortunately for America, our country is surrounded by oceans to our east, west, and southeast borders. To our north is Canada, who respects the sovereignty of our respective borders.

Unfortunately, along the remaining southern border, we have Mexico, whose citizens and those citizens who cross into Mexico from Central America enter our country illegally with ease and most certainly do not respect our borders or sovereignty.

We should be clear here. Mexico is complicit in this illegal entry and does little, if nothing, to restrict this illegal entry into our country.

Mexico has very strict restrictions on illegal entry into their country, but their behavior with respect to our southern border is very different.

I want to state very clearly, for those that may distort my assertions, that I am not suggesting that we go to war with Mexico or any other country in the region over this problem.

However, I do believe that America has to be very firm with Mexico in solving this problem and exert all the pressure available to us to persuade Mexico to act as a responsible neighbor.

Have you ever wondered why the Mexican government does not do anything to assist us or even express a willingness to prevent this illegal crossing?

Let's think about the possible reasons.

Ask yourself, of the people that are here illegally, how many have found work? And where are they spending that income?

Please keep in mind that if someone is here illegally and has found work, it is again illegal on the part of the person or company that hires this person, which is another subject we will speak to later in this chapter.

In most cases, these people are paid in cash, and if so, they are not paying taxes, which is another problem that harms our country.

But where are they spending the money earned? I suggest that the greater amount of this income is sent back to family members or friends in Mexico or other countries of origin.

I would also suggest that many that are here legally through existing laws, such as guest worker programs, also send most of their earnings back to Mexico, but at least this income is taxed. Or is it?

So you see, Mexico is content in not doing anything to assist us with these illegal crossings of our border and wants as many guest worker visas issued as possible.

This flow of US dollars back to Mexico only helps their economy, so why would they do anything that stop this? They wouldn't!

A second reason may be due to the fact that Mexico would prefer to see its citizens cross our borders so they relieve the stress on their public services, especially those who have committed crimes.

Mexico's standard of living for most of their citizens is very low compared to that of America. This, along with the corrupt nature of their federal and local governments, continues to fail many Mexicans.

This same failure repeats itself throughout Central America, so is it any wonder that we have so many desperate people attempting to cross our southern border with Mexico?

One last point on Mexico is its inability to eliminate the drug cartels who play a large part in the country's corruption. These drugs, in large numbers, continue to enter our country unchecked through our unsecured southern border.

This not only is harmful to the health of our country but also places a great deal of strain and costs on our various law enforcement agencies.

So let's think back to the importance of national sovereignty and the effect this open border can have.

Would we ever allow a collapse of our US Coast Guard and leave our shores unprotected to invasion by a foreign enemy?

Would we ever do the same with our northern border with Canada and leave that border unprotected?

Of course we wouldn't!

So why in the world do we allow this breach to our national sovereignty and security to continue unchecked with our border with Mexico?

Will it surprise you when I say that it is again political? It shouldn't!

The politicization of this crisis is solely due to the same dysfunction of our national politicians, both Republican and Democrat, as described in earlier chapters. They each have reasons why they want this influx of illegal aliens to continue.

But both parties and their reasons are rooted in politics and not in the best interest of America. We also have a large number of activists who promote this illegal entry and insist on distorting this illegal entry as innocent immigration by those seeking a greater standard of living.

And of course we have many in the media who distort this crisis in order to support those who support this illegal crossing into our country.

Your resistance to the targeted thought by others must be at its greatest when thinking through this crisis.

With respect to the open nature of this border, you will hear many excuses, such as "it is not possible to secure the entire border" or "it is not possible to build a wall or fence to secure this border."

This is only deception, which is a tactic used by these national politicians over and over again to distract America from the real issues and achievable solutions.

Remember my comments on how politicians will overcomplicate an issue in order to validate their many excuses for not fixing the problem.

Think about it. This border is approximately two thousand miles in length. Do you not think it can be secured?

More than forty-five years ago, this country undertook the notion to send a man to the moon, and in 1969, an American took the first steps on the surface of the moon.

This vision and belief in America's greatness was initiated by JFK, a true leader. Sadly, our current president does not possess this type of leadership ability.

So are we to believe that with today's technology and American ingenuity, we cannot create a secure fence, whether it be physical or virtual, along with increased border agents where it might be necessary in some stretches of this border?

Without a doubt, we can, and we could do it very quickly.

Americans know this and have become frustrated with our national politicians, especially with our president and the lack of willingness to act in America's interest.

Make no mistake, we have a silent invasion of this border taking place, meaning those rushing across this border are not doing so with guns blazing but are still invading our country.

Some may believe that the word "invasion" is an exaggeration of this problem. It isn't!

These people that are crossing our border are infringing on every American's right to a secure nation. Those crossing are also seeking to take advantage of America's freedoms, public services, and opportunities.

These freedoms and benefits belong to every American and those here legally and not anyone else, regardless of their plights. We must resist the temptation to think of this in only a humanitarian way and not as the true threat that it is.

Additionally, we look foolish and weak as a nation to the rest of the world in our ineptitude to secure this border.

It is only a matter of time before those who truly wish to kill Americans find the way to exploit this open border and do great harm to our American way of life.

Do not be fooled by those who understate the possibility that this can occur. It is already happening when you consider the extent of drug and human trafficking that is taking place with ease across this border.

Also, we know many of these people crossing our border are criminals, guilty of serious crimes, such as murder and rape, and sadly, they have committed this same type of violence against innocent American citizens.

So again, with all of this said, why are we not securing this border?

How can the greatest nation on earth allow this to happen?

It is due to the incompetence of the same entrenched politicians we spoke of in the last chapter. Without the correct political will, this problem cannot be fixed.

Every American must demand that this breach in our national security be corrected immediately and loudly express disappointment at every opportunity— and certainly at the ballot box!

In the prior chapter, I spoke about a candidate running in the 2016 presidential contest embracing and self-imposing term limits and how successful that candidate would be in winning the presidency.

If that same candidate would also commit unconditionally to secure this border, he or she would bring even greater certainty to winning the presidency.

It is essential that we secure this border and treat it with the same security measures and importance as our other borders. This must be done before any honest discussion or compromise on immigration can take place.

Now let's discus the second point of this chapter, immigration.

As we discuss it, is absolutely critical that we inform ourselves on how serious a crisis this is and the serious consequences of allowing it to continue.

Let's try to take the emotion out of our thought analysis for a moment, which is why I stated earlier that this crisis is probably more politicized than the other crises talked about in this book. By emotion, I do not mean compassion or concern when thinking through immigration.

However, with only emotions, and without clear and honest thought, we will continue to allow the overpoliticization of this crisis to distract America from the true nature of the problem that confronts us.

It is important to understand that an open border with Mexico is simply a means to ensure an end result that many politicians use to accomplish their goal of unchecked entry into our country.

It is also important to understand that our current president and his Democratic Party and those who support it, along with many in the media, greatly distort this American crisis. The Republican Party also distorts this crisis but not in such a divisive way.

I believe that the Democratic Party believes this unchecked entry of illegal aliens will lead to a reliable voting bloc and a way to deceive American citizens of a Mexican or Latino heritage that the Republican Party only wishes to discriminate against them and those wishing to immigrate here.

I also believe that those in the Republican Party look the other way on this crisis, with the intent to appease business donors that look to this illegal entry as a means of cheaper labor.

While I do believe the Republican Party is just as responsible as the Democratic Party for not solving this crisis, I do feel that there are some in the Republican Party that are honestly trying to find ways to secure this border and deal with immigration in the best interest of America.

By some, I am not referring to the current leaders in the Republican Party that only give lip service when speaking to this problem.

These same entrenched politicians in both parties have not only overpoliticized this issue but overcomplicated it as well.

Additionally, our president has chosen to not enforce some of the current immigration laws and has instituted unlawful immigration measures through abusing the executive order power of his presidency.

I would ask you to consider the following question very carefully. Are these politicians, our president included, really concerned with the well-being of these illegal aliens?

They are simply using these people as a means to a political end with interest only in their own agendas and ambitions, and certainly not with any great humanitarian concern.

However, in their attempt to deceive us, they distort their comments and attitudes to appear as if they really care about the human element to this problem.

Remember the recurring statement "this is not who we are as Americans" that many use when trying to convince Americans that they are on the correct side of a crisis, when in reality they are only trying to target and influence our thought through emotion and a twisted view of patriotism.

America cannot be the America we love and cherish unless we place Americans first. It is that simple.

We have to be honest that, yes, these are fellow human beings, but crossing our border at will violates our national sovereignty and therefore is illegal.

This illegal action is threatening the well-being of America and every American citizen, as well as noncitizens who are here legally and that have followed our immigration laws.

So let's stop with all the distraction, distortion, division, and emotion and discuss this crisis in a pragmatic, honest, unified, and calm way that produces an American solution.

This crisis further highlights the need for America to take back Washington and rid ourselves of the corruption that is eroding our political system, limiting our ability to deal with this issue.

Let's now think about the causes today that encourage and allow illegal entry in to our country.

First and most obvious is the unsecured nature of our southern border. This in itself is as if we had a great beacon in our southern sky that shouted, "Come on in whenever you like!"

So yes, let's do what is best for America and secure it now!

Our immigration crisis is not only caused by the openness of our southern border but also by other failures.

As mentioned earlier, our president chooses to ignore many of the immigration laws already in place. He has also used his executive power to unlawfully change the status of many illegal aliens that are here, allowing them to come forward without the fear of deportation.

This is nothing more than an attempt to find a pathway for the millions of people here illegally to bypass our lawful immigration and naturalization process.

The ultimate goal of our president, his party, and other supporters is to bestow the right to vote on those that have crossed our border illegally, which they believe will create a reliable Democratic voting bloc.

At the time of writing this book, this executive order has been challenged in court, has been blocked, and is now under appeal.

So you see, there is no leadership coming from Washington on this crisis. These actions by our president and those that support him serve only as a catalyst for those who wish to come to America; they can do so illegally and without fear of deportation.

Please remember, as I have pointed out in earlier chapters, that many of our politicians, including our president, prefer a state of crisis and confusion when confronting the challenges that face America.

They believe a crisis makes it easier to deceive and alarm America, which allows them to advance their policies quickly and without adequate debate and analysis.

They are not interested in what everyday Americans think about this crisis. As always, they are only concerned with their own personal agendas and ambitions.

In many cases, their deception only widens the crisis and pushes the proper solution further and further from reach.

Our southern border states have tried various measures to stop the illegal crossings and limit public services to those here illegally but are blocked by the federal government time and time again.

Immigration falls to the federal government for policy and enforcement, so if ignored by those in Washington only creates greater chaos and stress for those bordering states.

Every tax dollar that a state spends on immigration enforcement, in instances where the federal government should be enforcing laws, not only puts undue stress on a state's budget but should make us wonder what is happening with our tax dollars to fund these various federal agencies tasked with immigration enforcement.

I do not believe that anyone truly knows the number of illegal aliens in our country at this time, but we usually hear between ten and fifteen million. It is likely much higher, but even if it were just ten million, is that not very alarming?

Those here illegally are not just huddled in place and hiding in our southern border states. Many have moved to different states across America. Many states and cities have wrongfully created sanctuaries with incentives that attract many illegal aliens.

This only creates more confusion and barriers to our local authorities' willingness to work with federal immigration and enforcement authorities to properly address those here illegally.

Many states offer taxpayer-provided services to those here illegally, such as public assistance and education. Our health care delivery is also used by those here illegally.

All of these benefits are simply free, meaning that those here illegally are not paying taxes and therefore should not be entitled to any assistance and benefits. It only rewards their lawlessness.

Remember my earlier mention of those here illegally who are violent criminals. Not only does this unnecessarily threaten our safety, but think of the tremendous cost to prosecute and incarcerate these criminals!

This is further highlighted by the instances where violent criminals, after committing violent crimes, serve time and then after being deported simply walk back across our border and again commit violent crimes in this country.

In some cases, this happens multiple times by the same person!

All of this creates unnecessary strain to these states' budgets and continues to raise the taxes for Americans and those here legally.

Many states are struggling to balance their budgets, and many Americans are suffering as a result of an overburdened condition within their various state agencies, which only they should be entitled to!

Don't you find it ridiculous when you hear those that support this unlawful entry into our country make foolish statements such as, "This is the right thing to do, and how could we look the other way when there are so many children affected?"

What about America's children and the children of those here legally?

As we approach the primaries for the 2016 presidential race, we hear more and more about the term "anchor babies" and the Fourteenth Amendment to our constitution.

This discussion is of course distorted by many politicians and those who support illegal entry.

The term "anchor babies" refers to the children of illegal aliens who are born while they are in this country illegally. These children are considered legal residents at birth by those who wish to stretch the rights established in the Fourteenth Amendment.

These same politicians and those who support illegal entry also believe that these babies born to illegal alien mothers within US borders are called anchor babies because, under the 1965 Immigration Act, they act as an anchor that pulls the illegal alien mother and eventually a host of other relatives into permanent US residency.

We have many in politics and those that self-describe as constitutional experts interpret the Fourteenth Amendment differently and are driven by varying political views.

I will not attempt to convince anyone that I am a constitutional scholar, because I am not. However, as an American citizen, I have read this amendment and listened to the various arguments on both sides of this debate.

I do not believe this amendment guarantees the rights of citizenship to babies born of those here illegally.

The real contention is over the words in Section 1 of the Fourteenth Amendment that states "all persons born or naturalized in the United States, and subject to the jurisdiction thereof, are citizens of the United States and the state wherein they reside."

I strongly encourage my readers to spend time reading and understanding not only the amendment itself but the amendment's authors and their rationale for proposing it. They also clearly stated at the time that it did not include those born here of illegal aliens.

Please also consider the wrong it was trying to correct when adopted back in 1868.

I would also ask you to take notice of those who disagree with my assertion and that of many Americans in how they craft their deceptive statements to promote their beliefs that the Fourteenth Amendment does grant citizenship to those born here of illegal aliens.

They would have you believe that we are acting as radicals in defying our constitution and should seek to amend it rather than oppose it.

This is the same distraction and deception that they regularly use as a means to accomplish their personal and political agendas without not any concern for a true American agenda!

This amendment does not need to be changed; it simply needs to be interpreted properly with American wisdom.

Lastly on this subject, the US Supreme Court has not ruled on this matter specifically, but some have tried to distort and state that it has ruled specifically on this issue.

However, if it did come before our US Supreme Court, one can only imagine how they would rule, given how politicized this court has become.

I did not want to spend this much time on the subject of anchor babies, but it is very important to see that it does create another incentive for illegal entry into our country.

I believe it highlights the absurdity of those who argue that the acceptance of anchor babies is legal and good for America.

As we continue to examine our country's immigration, I would like to stress that those who always speak to "comprehensive immigration reform" and feel it should include those millions currently here illegally and securing our southern border are wrong.

We should not have to consider and debate new laws or changes to existing laws because our leaders have failed to safeguard our sovereignty and have not secured this border or quickly deport illegal aliens before they can root their way into American communities.

When those who support illegal entry into this country speak of comprehensive immigration reform, what they really mean is ignore the border, allow continued illegal entry, quickly legalize the illegal aliens already here, and pass legislation to expedite naturalization of those same people.

This is a disingenuous approach and should be rejected, as including border security is only a ploy to deceive America that they are we really concerned about this unchecked and unlawful entry into our country. They are not!

We should not believe for a minute that, with current state of political dysfunction in Washington, a comprehensive immigration reform type of approach is even possible, but most importantly it is not necessary.

It is so obvious that the correct path and first step is to immediately secure this border with a permanent structure and, while doing so, deploy the appropriate amount of manpower in law enforcement and our National Guard in the areas most prone to illegal crossing.

Think back to Mexico and their resistance to assist in restraining this illegal entry and ask yourself, how much in foreign aid do we send annually to Mexico?

In 2013, for example, we gave Mexico over $51 million in aid. Why would we continue this unless they cooperate fully with us to restrict this unlawful entry?

We should cut this off immediately until they comply.

We should also consider trade restrictions as well, unless or until Mexico does more to act as a responsible neighbor.

The frustrating aspect of this crisis is that, with the current political leadership, it is almost impossible to have any real change and honest debate until we elect the next president.

However, if America comes together and insists that Congress act to secure this border now, we may see some results. But we have to speak so loudly that those standing for reelection in 2016 realize that if they do not act now, they will not receive anywhere near the majority of votes to retain their respective offices.

This is why I stated earlier that a candidate running for the presidency in 2016 must not speak to this crisis broadly but speak very specifically, loudly, and repeatedly about the need for Congress to act now on securing this border, rather than wait and continue to make excuses.

While I believe the Republican Party is just as responsible as the Democratic Party for this crisis, I do believe that some of the current Republican candidates running for the presidency in 2016 have expressed serious concern regarding securing the border.

Also, with a current Republican majority in the House and Senate, it is more likely for a Republican candidate to advance this action rather than a candidate from the opposing party.

This will expose those in Congress who ignore the need to secure the border and only offer the same tired excuses. Congress can and must appropriate the funding needed to finally secure this border.

In 2006, the Secure Fence Act was passed to secure seven hundred miles of this border, yet less than one hundred miles is actually secured with a double-layer fence, which was the original intent of this act.

Examine closely any claims of a greater number of miles that are secured, as our government includes vehicle barriers and vehicles in their current estimates of how much of the border is secured through fencing.

Our current president has frozen the development and deployment of the virtual fence component of this act. Any surprise?

The current Congress must also hold the Department of Homeland Security and its current secretary responsible for this border securement, and if he refuses to comply, they should remove him through impeachment.

The American people must watch this process closely and punish those who vote no or those who skip or try to block this vote, with a no vote for all of those seeking reelection in 2016.

Once passed, it will likely be vetoed by the current president, but we must insist that Congress override the veto, and again, all of those who do not vote or skip the vote to override his veto will receive a no vote when they next stand for reelection.

We need new leaders who will challenge these entrenched politicians in both political parties in the House and Senate in the 2016 primary elections for their offices.

Simply stated, enough is enough with this issue of border securement.

The number of illegal aliens currently here is not only due to the openness of our southern border. We have many that overstay their nonimmigrant visas, such as those for tourists, temporary workers, and students.

The length of time allowed to stay varies among the different types of visas issued. We also issue border crossing cards for those crossing from Canada and Mexico.

Additionally, we allow entry for those from countries where we participate in a visa waiver program for those traveling as tourists and for business.

The actual number of those overstaying these nonimmigrant visas and other programs is not known. However, it does vary based on the type of visa or program.

Government and research groups' estimates vary, but you often hear that between 25 and 40 percent of those here illegally have overstayed their visa or other border crossing programs.

When you closely listen to why this is happening, you hear over and over again that we cannot adequately match entry and exit of those holding visas, so we cannot be sure who has overstayed and is now here illegally.

You also hear that this is not so much of a problem for those traveling here by air and sea but is much more of a problem for those crossing our land borders, and that the length of stay allowed also creates problems in tracking these visas.

This failure by our government to control and prevent overstays is just as ridiculous as our inability to secure our southern border. After the 9/11 attacks, we found that several of the hijackers had overstayed their visas.

Supposedly this was the wakeup call for government to act and implement a state-of-the-art system to match entry and exit for all those that held legal status to come here on a temporary basis.

This has not happened, and again, it is due to the incompetence of those in Washington and their desire to follow other agendas instead of an American agenda to solve these problems.

Think about it. With today's technology, such as biometric identification and the ability to quickly transmit data via the Internet, it should be easy to accomplish a reliable system of matching entry and exit, if we have the will!

Also, if we had this system in place, think about how easy it would be to identify those overstaying their visas, if we implemented biometric identification at certain points where those here illegally try to gain access, benefit from America, or interact with law enforcement.

This would not infringe on our liberty and freedom as Americans, as this initiative is only to identity and match those IDs of those here illegally, if they were registered properly through biometric identification when first entering this country.

It should be unthinkable that the greatest nation on this planet and with supposedly the brightest minds in IT cannot solve this problem.

Ask yourself, if a system of government is failing and harming America, would you allow it to continue and accept excuse after excuse, or would you simply shut it down until it is fixed?

My desire would be to temporarily suspend and limit immigration until this is resolved. Sure, I know immediately that those who support illegal entry would shout loudly about the harm it would cause, and those that rely on tourism from other countries would object.

But think about the harm and cost to our nation by not addressing it!

Again, my intent is to limit immigration and slow it down until we have an immigration policy in America's interest, not in the interest of those wishing to come here.

We must put America first!

Immigration should be a means to enhance a country's prosperity, not diminish it—and certainly not putting the interests of those wishing to come here over those of American citizens and those currently here legally and seeking naturalization.

America has nothing to be ashamed of with respect to immigration and our generosity, as we have for several years now issued on average each year one million resident visas (ten-year green cards) and, we naturalize nearly the same annually.

The fact that America is the most prosperous and freest nation in the world is not a reason to allow endless immigration, and we should not allow anyone or any group or any other nation to demand different of us!

Another concern and reason for slowing immigration is to allow for the proper assimilation of those that have immigrated here legally, which is absolutely critical to America's future. It will keep this country America and not let it become a large mass of subsets of other nations without any national unity.

We have to realize that the greatness of America is at risk if we allow immigration without the necessary assimilation that adopts American values and beliefs, which is the only way for America to replicate its greatness for generations to come.

The percentage of those here who are foreign born compared to those US born is rising. Think carefully about this. Is this healthy for America?

We have to be very thoughtful here and remember that America's greatness is rooted in the loyalty of its citizens to America and no other nation.

Yes, each of us has a proud heritage, and we should not forget that our parents and grandparents emigrated here from countries around the globe. But our hearts and minds must belong to America, which creates American patriotism, which is like no other nation in the world!

Along with America's great freedoms and liberty for its citizens comes a serious challenge, as with these freedoms, we easily allow illegal aliens to root themselves in our society, and unless they engage in criminal activity, they are not easily identified as being here illegally.

Ask yourself, why do many of our state and federal agencies provide documents and instructions in not only English but Spanish? Is this not helping many of those here illegally from Latin America to continue unchecked and unjustly take advantage of America's greatness?

Of course it is. We should stop it and insist that English be the only language with respect to our state and federal governments and not facilitate those who choose not to learn and accept English.

As I stated earlier, each of us are very proud of our individual heritage, and many of us speak more than one language, and that's fine, but if you wish to come here legally and become an American, the only acceptable language is English.

We know that a majority of those here illegally are of Hispanic descent. We also know that those of Hispanic decent that have resident status or those who have been naturalized comprise a growing percentage of the US population.

Therefore, we have to be very vigilant when thinking about this and the potential damage it can have on the American fabric. Closely listen to those in favor of this unchecked entry across our southern border and their eagerness to legalize and naturalize those here illegally.

My concern is that we may be undergoing a silent invasion right before our eyes by those who wish to change America and refuse to assimilate to our culture and values, instead embedding their culture and values into American Society!

As we close this chapter, I want to spend some time on another incentive to those who wish to violate our sovereignty, most specifically those coming across our southern border.

The incentive is that many now know they can find work, even if here illegally, as many US companies, small and large, will hire them.

Again, this is the result of our federal government's incompetence and failure to act responsibly and leverage American technology and ingenuity.

I am sure many of you have heard the term E-Verify along with the I9 form, which are meant to verify employment eligibility to legally work in the United States. While E-Verify has had success, it still has problems with employers adhering to its use and other disconnects.

I do not believe we have a lack of technology solutions but rather a lack of political will to enact and then enforce the solutions.

Additionally, we have an underground economy in our country, meaning we have company and individual employers paying their workers in cash and not reporting their wages or paying related income taxes. This is just another incentive for those to cross our border illegally, and it makes it easier for those who knowingly hire those here illegally to operate their businesses.

As much as this is illegal on the part of these employers and does harm to our country and should be corrected, we must also recognize that our government makes it very difficult for small businesses to survive.

Please consider the large number of Americans and those here legally that are unemployed. You may have heard of the labor participation rate, which measures the number of people sixteen years and older who are able to work. It has fallen dramatically and continues to drop. At the time of writing this book, it is approximately 62.5 percent.

The national unemployment rate is approximately 5.5 percent, which is not truly the number, and this metric continues to be distorted by our government.

Our poverty rate continues to rise, as well as the number of those on public assistance in one form or another.

Think about these alarming facts very carefully! Why would we even consider immigration of any sort until we address the employment and social needs of America?

Don't be fooled by those who distort these facts and say there are many Americans who won't perform the work available, and therefore those jobs are taken by those coming here legally as well as illegally.

These are the same people that promote limitless government and state dependency programs that do not provide any incentives or pathways for those unemployed or in poverty to lift themselves out of this endless cycle of despair.

Ask yourself, why we would continue these same policies regarding our immigration strategy when it is obvious that this country cannot continue to absorb the high numbers immigrating here legally? When added to the high numbers of illegal aliens, it will only continue to erode America's prosperity.

After the great surge of lawful immigration between 1880 and 1920, in the period between 1925 and 1965, we did limit immigration into our country.

Look at the positive results of that pause and how those that immigrated here during this surge period successfully assimilated into America—and then how those born here of those same immigrants created one of the greatest generations in our nation's history.

Just like with other crises talked about in this book, you will have to be on guard to recognize all the distortion and distraction by those in politics and the media who have no interest in solving this crisis but only in pursuing personal or political agendas.

You may have noticed that throughout this chapter I have only referred to those here illegally as "illegal aliens," not as "illegal immigrants," not as "undocumented immigrants" and not as "citizens in waiting" or any other ridiculous politically correct reference.

The solutions to this crisis are very simple, but our politicians, activists for illegal entry, and those in the media who support them will dispute this assertion and will only complicate this crisis, which is an all too common tactic they use to deceive America.

As I have stated before, I firmly believe in American correctness and the wisdom of America to solve this crisis, and I encourage my readers to embrace their important role in solving this crisis.

America, please step forward, as we must solve this crisis!

# Chapter 8

# Now What?

Great question—but one that has many answers!

Have you ever considered what is in your *thought toolbox*? Let me explain.

We process thoughts in many different ways, as we discussed in chapters 1 and 2, and then our thought processes affect our perspectives and actions.

Our thought toolboxes can be very basic, meaning that we just allow our thought processes to occur without any real examination of what is causing the thoughts we have, and then we form our opinions and actions.

Conversely, some of us possess thought toolboxes that are much more discerning, meaning we apply varying degrees of analytical examination of what enters our consciousness and the thoughts it creates, which of course guides our actions that follow.

I encourage of each of you who possesses only a basic thought toolbox to upgrade your toolbox to one that will enable you to apply more examination of the thoughts you process.

This upgrade will not be the same for everyone, and I am sure some will say they do not need any change in their thought analysis.

You may be correct with respect to many of life's daily experiences, but when considering the major crises facing our nation, and certainly the ones I cite in this book, you will need an upgrade.

The upgrade I am speaking of is nothing more than a conscious decision to find the time in our busy lives to consider our thought processes and these crises in a way we have never done before.

We must find the catalyst that will convince us that we need to rethink how we prioritize our thought processes and then allocate sufficient time to reach objective thought and outcome.

I hope this book and the crises discussed will help to provide that catalyst.

Please keep in mind the focus on politics in this book and how we process all of the incoming political news and often just accept it as factual. We must understand that there is little fact in most of the political news we encounter.

This is not only due to a great bias in many of our news outlets, but as we have discussed in this book, our political system, especially at the national level, is corrupt and unworthy of our trust.

Ask yourself when you feel the most informed. Is it when you simply listen to others and their opinions, or is it when you search out your own sources and answers and then form your opinions?

I believe that most of us would state the latter.

We do this every day, some more than most, in varying degrees. However, when it comes to politics and by extension the management of our country, we all too often don't.

So a vital part of your thought-toolbox upgrade is to ensure you consider politics on a much more frequent basis.

Let me also stress that many of us who possess complicated or highly technical thought toolboxes may need upgrades as well when considering the politics of our nation.

After reading this book, I would encourage you to strongly consider your approach to thought and politics and then read this book a second time.

My goal is not to convince you to allow politics to consume every aspect of your day but rather to convince you to take a more proactive role in our country's politics and the governing of our nation.

But we have to choose the right leaders!

Our constitution grants to us our right to vote. As we age, we should never forget the enormous leverage this provides to us and never, absolutely never, fail to exercise this right and privilege!

Additionally, we should never underestimate the value of this single vote when we are considering whether or not to participate in the election process of a public official or any other ballot issue.

Remember—those who seek to influence our vote with deception and dishonesty would rather we not vote if they cannot be assured of our vote.

For those of us in despair and unable to find meaningful work, please do not cast your vote for any politician, either local or national, who promises to give you more assistance if you vote for him or her.

This may sound convincing, considering your personal circumstances, but in reality, your vote for these politicians will only continue to grow government and make you more invisible to these same dishonest politicians!

Ask yourselves, as the government continues to grow, which it has dramatically, why haven't the levels of poverty and unemployment dropped?

These same politicians try to convince us that if they raise taxes on companies and those individuals at higher income levels, government will then help those of us in despair.

The truth is that the more the government taxes, the larger it becomes. It will only continue its wasteful spending and nothing more!

Sadly, our local and federal governments fail to even find the ways to ensure our safety in many of our neighborhoods and communities, which is the result of these same failed politicians!

The larger government becomes, the smaller America becomes.

Please understand that waiting for the state and federal governments to provide benefits and doing nothing else will only hold us in place and not provide any opportunity for us to grow and move out of poverty and despair.

Government does not provide opportunity, only dependency!

The only way we can lift ourselves out of poverty is through hard work and personal responsibility, which will provide us with a pathway to greater prosperity.

That awful job we take today may be very difficult, but we should use it as the motivation to work even harder, which will enable us to find that next great job that will propel us forward and allow us to fully participate in America's greatness.

So I ask those who find themselves in poverty to resist this tendency to vote for those who only make promises and seek to grow government, and to instead consider those who inspire and seek to reduce government.

This also applies to those who are working and supporting families, living paycheck to paycheck, or those who do not feel they can accomplish much more.

For those who feel they are doing well, growing families, experiencing many of life's pleasures, having great jobs and good incomes, they too must resist the tendency to vote for big government.

Those doing well may not truly understand that many of our fellow Americans are being left behind and falling into an endless cycle of poverty and crime because of a dysfunctional government that will not change unless we force it to change.

Our government in Washington is consumed with politicians concerned with their personal enrichment rather than enriching America!

Yes, I know, we all have our hands full with all of life's challenges, but please take more time to carefully consider whom you are voting for and why.

I can assure you that if we take these initiatives in the short term, we will solve these crises and reestablish a government for its citizens, which will be immune to the corruption we see today.

These actions will free us from having to deal with it again and allow every American, and I mean every American, to enjoy the greatness of this nation.

We must enact term limits and settle for nothing less.

We must speak so loudly that our voices will shake the halls of Congress and send the message to these failed politicians that their days in office are truly numbered.

I would like to be able to title the next book I write *The Spoken Thought, America's Comeback*!